GLYNDŴ

GLYNDŴR'S WAY
Llwybr Glyndŵr

David Perrott

AURUM PRESS

Cyngor Cefn Gwlad Cymru
Countryside Council for Wales

Thanks

The Glyndŵr's Way National Trail Officer while this book was being compiled
was Rab Jones. Rab has now moved on to greater things, but I'd like to extend
my sincere thanks for all his help and advice. The task would never have been
completed without the help of Morag, my wife. From giving lifts to and from
all sorts of obscure locations at any time of the day, to assisting with the
historical research and checking the manuscript, her help has been beyond
measure. We have tried to thoroughly check everything but, if there are any
mistakes, they remain mine.

David Perrott, Darowen

First published in 2004 by Aurum Press Ltd ,
25 Bedford Avenue, London WC1B 3AT
in association with the Countryside Council for Wales

Text copyright © 2004 by David Perrott
The photographs on pages 43, 56, 62, 100, 104, 120 and 123 are by David Perrott
All other photographs copyright © 2004 by the Countryside Council for Wales

OS Ordnance Survey® This product includes mapping data licensed from Ordnance
Survey® with the permission of the Controller of Her Majesty's Stationery
Office. © Crown copyright 2004. All rights reserved. Licence number 43453U.

Ordnance Survey and Travelmaster are registered trademarks and the
Ordnance Survey symbol and Explorer are trademarks of Ordnance Survey,
the national mapping agency of Great Britain.

ISBN 1 85410 968 5

1 3 5 9 10 8 6 4 2
2004 2006 2008 2007 2005

Book design by Robert Updegraff
Printed and bound in Italy by Printer Trento Srl

Cover photograph: *The view north from Glyndŵr's Way overlooking Ceniarth Farm,
south-west of Talbontdrain, on the approach to Machynlleth.*
Title-page photograph: *The Fan Pool, near Llanidloes, from Glyndŵr's Way.*

CONTENTS

HOW TO USE THIS GUIDE

This guide to the 135-mile (217-kilometre) Glyndŵr's Way is divided into three parts:

- The Introduction, which explains the historical background to the trail and provides advice for walkers.
- Glyndŵr's Way itself, split into sixteen chapters, with maps accompanying the description for each route section. This part of the guide also includes information on places of interest and features of local merit. Key sites are numbered both in the text and on the maps to make it easier to follow the route description.
- The final part provides useful information on subjects such as local transport, accommodation and organisations involved with Glyndŵr's Way.

The maps have been prepared by the Ordnance Survey for this Trail Guide using 1:25 000 Explorer™ maps as a base. The line of Glyndŵr's Way is shown in yellow highlight, with the status, where known, of each section of the Way – footpath, bridleway or by-way, for example – shown in green underneath (see the key on the inside front cover). In some cases the yellow line on these maps does not coincide with the right-of-way indicated on the maps. Walkers should follow the yellow route in this guide, which is waymarked with the distinctive acorn symbol ♀ used for all National Trails, plus the Glyndŵr's Way waymarks.

The route is clearly described in the text, and important points to watch out for are marked with letters in each chapter, both in the text and on the maps. *Some maps start on a right-hand page and continue on the left-hand page – black arrows (➤) at the edge of the maps indicate the start point.*

Some sections of Glyndŵr's Way cross high, exposed and bleak moorland where mist is not uncommon. Should these conditions prevail while you are walking, a compass, and the ability to use it, will prove invaluable.

Distance Checklist

This will assist with planning your walk.

location	approx. distance from previous location	
	miles	km
Knighton	0	0
Cefn-suran	5 $^1/_2$	8.25
Llangunllo	1	1.6
Felindre	9 $^1/_4$	15
Llanbadarn Fynydd	7 $^1/_2$	12
Abbeycwmhir	8 $^1/_4$	13
Bwlch-y-Sarnau	3 $^1/_4$	5.25
Blaentrinant	3 $^1/_2$	5.75
Llanidloes	8 $^1/_2$	13.5
Afon Biga	9	14.5
Aberhosan	9 $^1/_4$	14.75
Talbontdrain	2 $^3/_4$	4.5
Machynlleth	6 $^3/_4$	10.75
Penegoes	2 $^1/_2$	4
Abercegir	4 $^3/_4$	7.5
Glantwymyn	4	6.75
Commins Gwalia	2 $^1/_2$	4
Llanbrynmair	4 $^1/_4$	6.75
Llangadfan	10 $^1/_4$	16.5
Llanwddyn	6 $^1/_2$	10.5
Pont Llogel	3 $^1/_2$	5.5
Dolanog	4 $^3/_4$	7.75
Pontrobert	3 $^1/_2$	5.5
Meifod	3 $^1/_2$	5.5
Welshpool	10 $^3/_4$	17.5

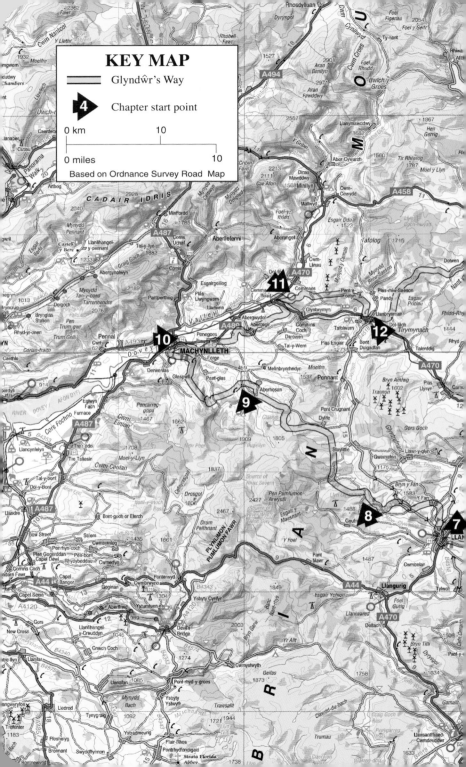

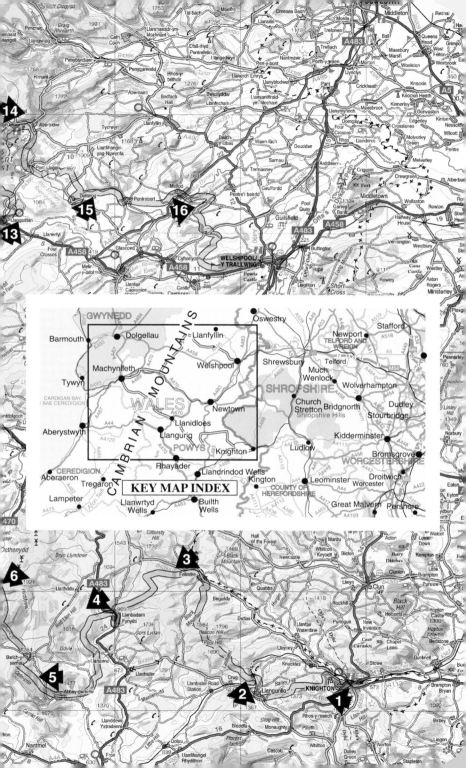

Preface

I was thrilled to participate in the opening of Glyndŵr's Way in Spring 2002 and to see it joining Offa's Dyke Path and Pembrokeshire Coast Path as the third member of the family of Welsh National Trails. Each National Trail has something special to offer and Glyndŵr's Way is no exception. The 135-mile (217-km) route passes through some of the best scenery in Mid Wales. From the beautiful isolation of Beacon Hill Common to the tranquillity of the banks of the River Vyrnwy; from the shores of Llyn Clywedog Reservoir to the rolling farmland of the Vale of Meifod – Glyndŵr's Way offers a superb walking experience.

Couple this with the rich variety of wildlife you will encounter along the route, add the historic and cultural associations of Owain Glyndŵr and the warm welcome of the people of Mid Wales and you have all the ingredients needed to make your experience of this new National Trail an exciting and memorable one.

John Lloyd Jones

John Lloyd Jones OBE
Chairman
Countryside Council for Wales

Rhagair

Roedd yn bleser o'r mwyaf cymryd rhan yn y dasg o agor Llwybr Glyndŵr yn ystod gwanwyn 2002, a'i weld yn dilyn ôl troed Llwybr Clawdd Offa a Llwybr Arfordir Sir Benfro fel y trydydd Llwybr Cenedlaethol yng Nghymru. Mae gan bob Llwybr Cenedlaethol rywbeth arbennig i'w gynnig, ac nid yw Llwybr Glyndŵr yn eithriad yn hyn o beth. Mae'r llwybr, sy'n 135-milltir (217-km) o hyd, yn eich tywys trwy rai o olygfeydd harddaf y Canolbarth. O unigedd bendigedig Comin Bryn Beacon i dawelwch glannau'r Afon Efyrnwy; o lannau Cronfa Ddŵr Llyn Clywedog i dir fferm bryniog Dyffryn Meifod – mae Llwybr Glyndŵr yn cynnig taith gerdded werth chweil.

Yn ogystal â hyn, fe gewch weld bywyd gwyllt o bob math, cewch sylwi ar y berthynas hanesyddol a diwylliannol ag Owain Glyndŵr, a chewch gyfle i flasu croeso cynnes trigolion y Canolbarth. Yn wir, dyma'r holl gynhwysion angenrheidiol ar gyfer gwneud eich taith ar hyd y Llwybr Cenedlaethol yma'n un gofiadwy a llawn cyffro.

John Lloyd Jones.

John Lloyd Jones OBE
Cadeirydd
Cyngor Cefn Gwlad Cymru

PART ONE

INTRODUCTION

Overlooking Raven Square Station, on the descent to Welshpool, viewed from the Llanerchydol Estate. From here it is just a short walk to the finish.

Glyndŵr's Way carves a very remote and beautiful 135-mile (217-km) arc that stretches through the hills and mountains of Mid-Wales between Knighton and Welshpool, anchored in the west by Machynlleth. This last town was, for a short while in the 15th century, declared the capital of Wales by Owain Glyndŵr, in a place which, to many eyes, was logically as central a situation for this institution as you can get in the Principality.

From the bleak but beautiful isolation of Beacon Hill Common to the tranquility of the River Vyrnwy, from the lonely moorland above Dylife to the rolling farmland of the Vale of Meifod, Glyndŵr's Way offers an exhilarating walking experience and a chance to explore the remote Mid Wales countryside. The route passes habitats which are nationally important, such as sessile oak woodland with carpets of bluebells, upland mire and heath, ancient hedgerows and unspoilt river valleys.

A particularly notable section is from Penfforddlas to Aberhosan, which bisects part of the Pumlumon massif noted for the extent and quality of its heather moorland, an increasingly rare habitat. Walkers on Glyndŵr's Way will also have the opportunity to observe at first hand the rich variety of wildlife typical of Mid Wales. Birds such as the skylark, buzzard and red kite are commonly seen along the route, and many lanes and hedge banks are rich with wildflowers, particularly in the spring. Mid Wales also remains a stronghold for the traditional pattern of small fields, whilst some sections of the Way pass through or close by common land, wind turbines and forestry, providing an insight into varying types of land management.

The original route of Glyndŵr's Way was created by Powys County Council in the mid-1970s. Following a report prepared for what was then the Countryside Commission for Wales (now the Countryside Council for Wales or CCW/Cyngor Cefn Gwlad Cymru) and Powys County Council, which recommended the creation of a National Trail, a Project Officer was appointed to develop a new route and one which would make much less use of tarmac surfaces. After consultation with landowners, local authorities and other interested parties, the new National Trail was finally opened in 2002. The route lies entirely within the county of Powys, which manages it on behalf of the CCW, with the latter body providing the majority of the funding for its upkeep.

Owain Glyndŵr

Who was Owain Glyndŵr? Perhaps his story has its roots in England's conquest of Wales, which was completed in 1284 under Edward I, when Prince Llywelyn was killed in a skirmish with English forces at Cilmery, near Builth Wells.

Owain ap Gruffydd, Owain Glyndŵr, was born around 1359, the son of Gryffydd Fychan and a descendant of the Royal House of Powys, and of Deheubarth, and also a distant relative of the Tudors. He probably served as an apprentice in law in London, staying at the Inns of Court. Later he became Squire to Henry Bolingbroke, King Richard's cousin, and during this period he learned his fighting skills, doubtless honed during campaigns in Scotland and Europe. Glyndŵr was one of the very few Welshmen who held estates from the Crown, and in 1398, his military career over, he settled on one of these estates near Sycharth in a moated wooden house with great halls and chambers. He married Margaret Hanmer and raised a 'nest of children' amidst orchards, fish ponds, peacocks and fallow deer. But all was not as peaceful as it seemed.

In the late 14th century there was discontent in Wales over punitive taxation and anti-Welsh legislation. The Black Death had left a legacy of poverty, destitution and unrest, and land was being enclosed by unscrupulous owners who wished to use it for profitable sheep farming. Tenant farmers were dispossessed by rent increases. In September 1399 Glyndŵr's neighbour, Sir Reginald Grey of Ruthin, stole some of his land and, although Glyndŵr tried to regain possession using legal means, the rift between the two men was deepened when Grey insulted Glyndŵr, saying 'What care we for barefoot Welsh dogs?'

Eventually Glyndŵr resorted to force to regain his land, and the spirit of rebellion quickly spread, with numerous attacks against English-owned property. The revolt grew, and soon English towns, and Abbeycwmhir, were attacked by bands of Welsh guerillas. The Covenant Stones, two quartz boulders at Hyddgen, high on Pumlumon, mark the spot were Glyndŵr defeated the Flemings in 1401 and, on 16 September, Owain was proclaimed Prince of Wales, encouraged by Welsh hatred for the English King Henry IV and his Marcher Lords. On 18 September Owain's motley army rode into Ruthin. By the 24th they had raided other towns and were closing upon Welshpool when they were routed near Shrewsbury. Henry's army arrived

Looking west from Castell-y-Blaidd on the wonderfully remote section between Felindre and Llanbadarn Fynydd. Castell-y-Blaid was probably abandoned when Castelltinboeth was built to the south-west.

the next day, and subsequently subdued the whole uprising. All of the rebels, except Owain, were pardoned.

This peace was, however, short lived and rebellion was rekindled when Henry IV passed onerous anti-Welsh legislation. Conwy Castle was burned and Owain raised a second army; Henry responded, strengthening garrisons and reinforcing castles. A comet which appeared in the sky in 1402 was taken as an omen, since its tail was said to point towards Wales, reinforcing Glyndŵr's reputation as a wizard. His second rebellion grew when he defeated the English at Pilleth, near Knighton, at a site called Bryn Glas. Owain then moved north, and blockaded the castles at Harlech and Caernarfon.

By 1404 Owain had secured Wales and established a Parliament in Machynlleth, and in 1406 the Tripartite Indenture

West of Glyndŵr's Way, from beneath Pegwn Mawr, which now has a sprawling wind far

the summit.

was signed. This was a pact between Glyndŵr, the Earl of Northumberland and Sir Edmund Mortimer, the most powerful of the Marcher barons, to divide England and Wales between them. He also tried to make an alliance with the French, but this came to nothing, even though he tried a second time, calling a meeting in Machynlleth and sending the famous Pennal Letter to Charles VI, King of France, in March 1406, expressing his wish to have a Welsh Church with bishops appointed from France rather than Canterbury, and to have two universities established, one in North and one in South Wales.

Eventually King Henry became ill, and Prince Henry, given a free hand to campaign in Wales, soon turned Owain into a fugitive. In 1407 the rebellion faded through starvation and a

The Montgomeryshire Canal in Welshpool, by Parc Howell, at the end of the walk. Although this section of the canal is navigable, it will be a few years before it links with the main waterways network.

lack of funds, and Aberystwyth and Harlech Castles, both held by Glyndŵr, were under siege. By 1409 they had fallen and in 1410 it was all over. Glyndŵr and his son Maredudd were forced to flee, living as guerillas.

What became of Owain Glyndŵr after 1412 is a matter of speculation. One early 20th-century author maintained he died on 20 September 1415 at Monnington-on-Wye. Others believe he ended his days at the home of his daughter Alice and her husband Hugh Scudamore at Monnington Stradell, in the Golden Valley in Herefordshire. But there are also those who hold that he went to live at Pwlliwrch, Darowen, near Machynlleth (just off Glyndŵr's Way, Chapter 10), and others who claim he died near Valle Crucis Abbey in Gwynedd.

Although Owain Glyndŵr's dream of independence ended in the early 15th century, he still remains an icon of Welsh culture, now reflected in the increasing confidence of 21st-century Wales, with its own fledgling parliament.

Planning your walk

Preparation is important so, if you have never tried hill walking, test yourself over a few days or weekends before deciding to take on Glyndŵr's Way. Many young people find they are naturally fit but lack stamina; older people still have the potential for excellent stamina but lack basic strength. It is never too late to get fit, but the older you are, the more gentle should be the programme. Some kind of exercise which makes you sweaty and breathless for 20 minutes every two or three days is an ideal level of preparation, to be built up gradually. If you can cope with this, a day or two on Glyndŵr's Way should hold no fears at all. However, to cope with the whole walk, day after day, requires extra stamina that can only be earned the hard way – on the hills.

To avoid blisters or sore feet, boots should be waterproof and thoroughly worn in, and socks should be absorbent, without lumpy seams. Hardening the skin on the soles and heels helps, and this can be assisted by applying alcohol or surgical spirit for a few weeks before a big walk. If blisters form, prick them and apply a porous plaster to keep the dead skin in place over the tender new layer underneath. Keep your toe nails clipped and make sure your boots fit properly.

Your first-aid kit should contain plasters, pain-relief tablets, something to treat diarrhoea, something to treat midge bites and

Looking east from the bare hill of Allt Dolanog towards Meifod, along the Afon Efyrnwy. Glyndŵr's Way follows the river virtually all the way to Pontrobert.

insect repellent. Lip salve can help wind-dried lips and Vaseline can help to soothe sore or chapped skin. It is best to know a little about first aid, and to be aware of the treatment for gastroenteritis (drink clear fluids with glucose and a little salt) and exposure (glucose, warm dry clothing and a quick walk to shelter).

Essential clothing for a day on Glyndŵr's Way should include a set of waterproofs (cagoule, overtrousers), a pair of warm trousers and a pullover. You may not need any of these items, but they should be packed in your rucksack, just in case. There is no need to invest in heavyweight mountain boots. Lighter walking boots with ankle support, to reduce the risk of sprained ankles, and a degree of waterproofing, are quite adequate. Fully enclosed gaiters (such as the Yeti type) and strong mountain boots will keep your feet dry even after a wet day above Dylife. A good waterproof rucksack is essential. Into this should go a compass, a Swiss Army knife or folding multi-tool, a couple of pencils and a set of appropriate maps, so don't forget this book!

Food and an adequate supply of drink (clean, plain water is probably best) and money complete the basic list, to which can be added a camera, mobile phone and charger, sunglasses (we live in hope!), notebook and whatever else you feel inclined to take with you. Company, or the deliberate avoidance of it, will of course be the nub of one of the most important decisions before the start of the walk. Safety, and making sure someone knows where you are, is even more important for lone walkers than it is for groups.

Anyone undertaking the whole walk will also need to think carefully about accommodation, for this will affect how much they carry and where they need to pick up provisions. Useful information on this and other topics appears on pages 163 to 168.

A note on Welsh terms

Although they are usually self-explanatory in the context, not all readers may be familiar with the following words commonly used in the text:

afon – river
bwlch – pass
cwm – valley
llyn – lake

PART TWO

GLYNDŴR'S WAY

1 Knighton to Llangunllo
Tref-y-Clawdd i Langunllo

6 ¹/₂ miles (10.5 km)

Knighton is known as Tref-y-Clawdd in Welsh, 'the town on the dyke': it was the English who called it 'Knight's Town' during the 17th century, when King Charles had his knights garrisoned in the area, although this name may have been a corruption of Cnwc-din, 'the fort on the hill spur'. The town has a colourful borderland history dating back at least to Caractacus, who is thought to have established a fortified settlement between Knighton and Clun to resist the Romans. Later King Offa of Mercia attempted to put a stop to the constant border disputes by building his dyke in the late 8th century. This substantial earthwork stretches from Treuddyn, north-west of Wrexham, in the north, to Chepstow in the south.

William de Braose built a wooden castle in Knighton in the 12th century, on a hill which became known as Bryn-y-Castell **1**, to discourage incursions by the Welsh, and this was followed by a sturdier stone-built structure to the east of Broad Street, and it was around this that the town developed. It was fittingly Owain Glyndŵr who conducted the last major assault on the town in 1402, when he defeated an English army at the Battle of Pilleth (Bryn Glas) and captured Sir Edmund Mortimer. A group of Wellingtonias planted in 1870 marks the site of a mass grave for the fallen. These events were presaged by the sighting of a comet over Europe in February of the same year, when the bards proclaimed Owain 'the son of prophecy'. Violent thunderstorms were attributed to his supernatural powers. In the midst of such violent events it is interesting to note that Edmund Mortimer and Owain Glyndŵr soon formed an alliance, which was bonded when Edmund married Glyndŵr's daughter. You can get a bus from Knighton to Pilleth – ring 01597 826678 for details.

Many of the buildings you will see in Knighton date from the 17th century, when it was an important trading and droving centre for east Radnorshire, and its prosperity increased due to its position on the Hereford to Montgomery and London to Aberystwyth roads. Indeed, in the late 18th century there were five tollgates around the town.

The Narrows, Knighton, at the start of Glyndŵr's Way. After Knighton, the next pub is in Llangunllo!

When the railway was built in 1860 it brought a new flush of prosperity as Knighton became a depot for seeds, fertiliser and feed, soon to be followed by tanning, malting and cloth production. St Edward's Church was substantially rebuilt in 1877 on the site of a Norman building, the remains of which survive in the lower part of the tower, which had been mostly demolished in 1756. The timbered belfry is particularly attractive: such structures are common amongst the churches of Herefordshire, and it is this which leads perhaps to the reason why this Welsh church should have an English dedication, but whether it is to Edward the Confessor or the Saxon King Edward the Martyr remains a matter of conjecture. If you fancy a pint, or a meal, there is no shortage of pubs and cafés in the town.

A commemorative stone by the clock-tower **A** at the junction of the High Street and Broad Street, built in 1872, now marks the start of Glyndŵr's Way and, as you begin your walk, climbing steeply up the hill, you will become increasingly aware of the town's snug position in the valley of the River Teme.

The High Street, or The Narrows, curves gently up to The Golden Lion in Market Street, where you turn left along Castle Road. Follow this as it bends to the right, giving a fine view down the valley to the left, and ahead. You continue along a narrow lane overlooking the town, eventually going steeply downhill. Cross a road and continue, maintaining your direction down a slightly narrower track. Continue walking beside back gardens and a corrugated iron fence, then pass Weaver's Cottages and carry on along the path. You are now walking beside a stream with trees all around, and the town has, for the moment, disappeared from view.

As a lane joins from the right at Mill Lodge, you fork right up a signed footpath, continuing ahead at the end of a cul-de-sac. Cross the road by Greenacre **B** and walk for a few strides up the driveway towards a house and then turn right just before Woodhouse Close. The narrow path climbs steeply, passing pretty back gardens. At the top of the hill cross a stile and turn right, walk ahead for 30 yards and then fork left in front of some houses. You can now enjoy a wonderful view over Knighton as you catch your breath.

Ignore a field gate to your right and continue along the green lane, walking around the northern side of Garth Hill and overlooking the valley. Ignore a stile to your right and continue ahead, and then ignore a path which heads uphill to your left and again continue ahead. Cross a stile and join a track which comes in from the right and then turn right following the track downhill (ignoring the track which climbs uphill). You are now walking through a very fine expanse of mixed deciduous woodland, crossing two stiles as you go, with views over the valley and the Heart of Wales Line **2,** where trains occasionally rumble by, and a fence to your right. Cross another stile, pass a little stile at the top of a path down to a house and continue along the main path, which now begins to curve left, leaving the beautiful Teme Valley and continuing around Garth Hill,

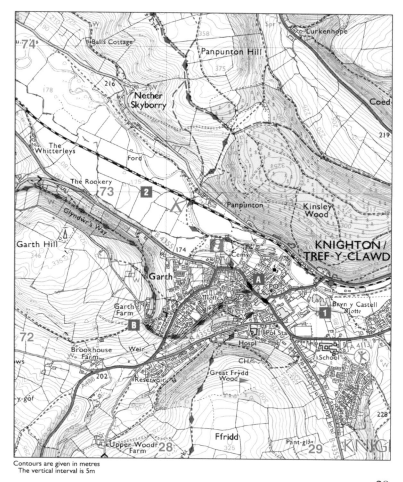

Contours are given in metres
The vertical interval is 5m

which rises high to your left. A single-track road approaches from the right, and the route of your track joins this **C**, and you continue ahead. When you meet another lane, turn left and follow this lane for a little under half a mile (800 metres). Before you reach the bottom of the hill, a track leaves to the right – follow this, going slightly uphill and passing Little Cwm-gilla Farm. The lane now climbs quite steeply between high banks, where you will find a few wild strawberries in early summer. It's a good idea to stop now and again to catch your breath, turning around to enjoy the fine view. You have earned it!

Walking on Bailey Hill, west of Knighton: already the countryside is wonderfully remote and the views breathtaking.

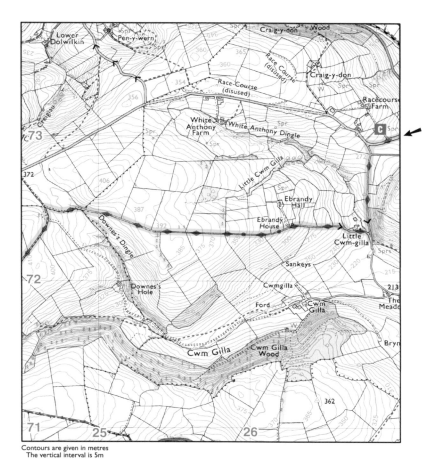

Contours are given in metres
The vertical interval is 5m

The tarmac is left behind at Ebrandy Hall as you continue walking ahead up the track for about a mile (1.6 km), still climbing! The track ends at the summit of Bailey Hill at a gate, which you go through. Continue with a fence and a hedgerow to your right. The view is now a full 360 degrees, and you should stop and savour it. You then descend the hill, beside a fence and a hedge, with an open view to the left as the track winds ahead up the next gentle hill. The track descends and you pass through a gate and continue ahead, soon beginning a gentle climb, with the hedge and the fence now to your left.

You reach a track and turn sharp left, to continue ahead when you reach a gate. You now cross a waymarked stile beside a gate and continue with the hedge on your left, starting

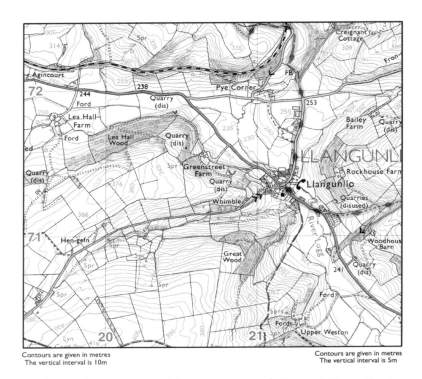

Contours are given in metres
The vertical interval is 10m

Contours are given in metres
The vertical interval is 5m

to descend once more with gentle, green hills tumbling off into the distance, and a clear ridge ahead. At the field corner continue ahead through a gate with the hedge still to your left. Descend by a small muddy pool and continue, with a fence to your left and lots of bright yellow gorse ahead. A large farmhouse appears. Go through a gate and continue ahead, with a quarry up the hill to your right. Ahead is a gate marked 'No Admittance'. About 10 yards before this gate turn left through a wooden gate **D** signed with a blue waymark indicating 'An Environmentally Sensitive Area'. Walk half-right downhill to a dumb waymark post, where you join a track and veer left to cross a small stream, then turn sharp right to walk beside the stream, following the track uphill. Go through a wooden gate, cross a stream and then turn right, to walk with the fence to your right. Go through a small wooden gate in the field corner, join the track ahead, cross a stream and veer left along the track by a waymark post. You pass a fishing pond to your left, and then go through a gate by a cattle grid, to leave the field and join a track which veers left.

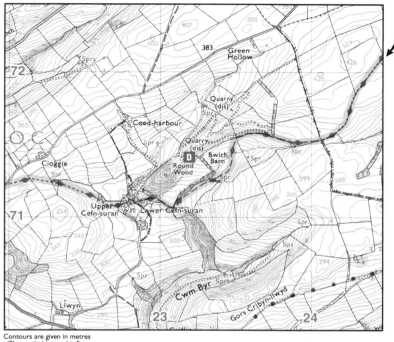

Contours are given in metres
The vertical interval is 5m

Enter the driveway of Cefnsuran and, directly ahead of the entrance to Cefnsuran, follow a waymarked path between trees by a tiny stream (don't turn left to walk around the house), which brings you to a stile. Cross this and immediately turn left and go through a gate. Walk across the yard and leave it via a waymarked gate along a track. You pass a duck pond, with rushes, and a man-made lake on the right and trees on your left before continuing ahead towards a stile. Ignore the green waymark and walk half-right to a stile, which you cross and turn left. Walk along the lane for 15 yards to a stile on your right. Cross it and walk ahead, downhill and through trees.

Soon you are following a little hollow pathway that descends into a quiet valley with trees all around. A waymark post appears ahead. Continue with trees on your left to reach a stile ahead, just across a farm track. Cross it and continue down the field. Go through a gateway in the bottom right-hand corner and continue ahead with a stream on your right. Cross a stile by a gate beside a garden and continue down the track beside a house to join a road where you turn right to reach Llangunllo.

Overlooking the outskirts of Knighton, with the Spaceguard Centre (until recently known

...e Powys Observatory) on the distant skyline. The Centre is open to visitors.

2 Llangunllo to Felindre

Llangunllo i Felindre

9 1/4 mile (15 km)

In Llangunllo village centre **A** turn right by The Greyhound pub **3**, which is also a community shop. This pub is really not to be missed: it is charmingly old fashioned, with a cosy roaring fire on chilly days, and a genial host. Go straight across the crossroads at the top and then, when the road curves to the right, go straight ahead through a gate and follow the path downhill to a little metal footbridge, and cross it. Now continue uphill, veering right and with a fence to your left. Go through a gate, and walk up to a road. Walk under the railway bridge and continue straight ahead along the track, crossing over a cattle grid (don't turn right along the road).

Pass Nayadd Fach and go through a gate to continue uphill along the track, going through a second gate. Just before you reach a yard and barn, go through a gate in front of you and continue with a hedge on your right. Go through a gate in the corner, after which there is a gate on your immediate left. Go through this and bear half-right to the top corner of the field, where you go through a gate to walk with a fence on your right. Go through a wooden gate and continue with a fence to the right. Go through another gate which leads onto a wide green track with a fence on either side. Eventually the track descends to join a farm road, where you veer right. At a cross-tracks continue ahead, beginning to climb. As you get higher, take time to stop now and again to catch your breath and look back to enjoy the view of the mountain ridges stepping away to the horizon. It is very typical of Mid Wales, with very few trees.

As you progress the track becomes wide and clear, crossing open moorland and you are, for the first time on Glyndŵr's Way, conscious of your elevated position. You steadily slog uphill until you pass between conifer plantations to reach a gate at the junction of several paths. Ignore the path to your right to go ahead for a few strides, then turn left **B** to cross Beacon Hill Common **4**. This is Crown Estate land, covering an area of 4,667 acres (1,890 hectares), and is administered by the Radnorshire Wildlife Trust. Walk with conifers on your left and

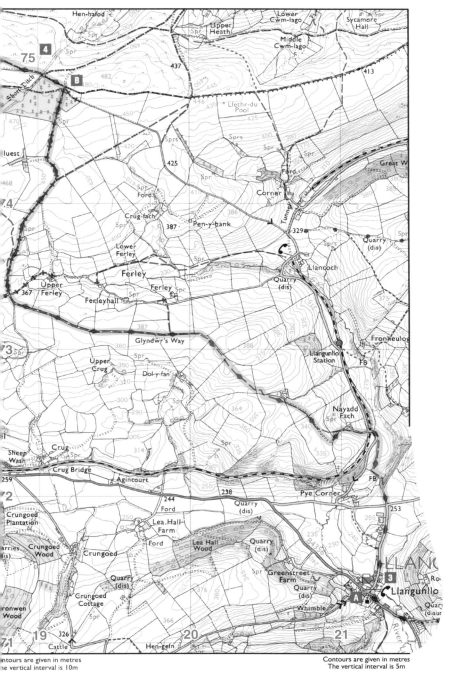

Hen-hafod
Upper Heath
Lower Cwm-Iago
Sycamore Hall
Middle Cwm-Iago

7.5 4
437
413

B
482
Llethr-du Pool

Short Ditch
Spr

luest
425
Great W
468
Ford
Corner
7.4
Ford
Crug-fach
Pen-y-bank
386
Tunnel
329
Quarry (dis)
Lower Ferley
Ferley
Llancoch
Upper Ferley
Ferley
Quarry (dis)
367
Ferleyhall
375
387
Glyndŵr's Way
388
Fronheulog
3 Spr
Upper Crug
Dol-y-fan
Llangunllo Station
FB
Nayadd Fach
Spr
364

Crug
Sheep Wash
Crug Bridge
Agincourt
255
238
FB
259
Pye Corner
253
2
244
Quarry (dis)
Crungoed Plantation
Ford
Lea Hall Farm
Ford
Lea Hall Wood
Quarry (dis)
arries is)
Crungoed Wood
Crungoed
Greenstreet Farm
LLAN
Ro
Quarry (dis)
Quarry (dis)
3
Llangunllo
ronwen Wood
Grungoed Cottage
376
Whimble
A
Qu (disu
71 19 326
20
21
River
Cattle
Hen-gefn

Contours are given in metres
The vertical interval is 10m

Contours are given in metres
The vertical interval is 5m

37

cross Short Ditch, an ancient earthwork, and continue. Soon you must veer to the right on the track, ignoring a gate to the left. Stay on the track for about 2 miles (3.2 km); it skirts around Pool Hill and gives lovely views along a valley to the right. Eventually the clear track ends, and you continue ahead along a green track as signed, surrounded by a wild expanse of heather upland with domed summits on each side. The track meanders on, gently rising and falling and offering the occasional glimpse of a side valley. As you approach Stanky Hill the track is again green and pleasant underfoot; and, as you approach its shoulder, a cwm comes into view ahead. Look out for the waymark post here which directs you to turn sharply right **C** along a less distinct, but still well-defined, track across the low ridge of the Black Mountain.

The track continues over the moorland for about 1½ miles (2.4 km), passing an isolated waymark post on the horizon. Follow the faint track as it descends, eventually reaching a bridge over a little stream, and continue to the right, now gently climbing with just sheep and moorland birds for company. The gentle climb uphill continues along a wide jumble of tracks, which soon condense into one clear track, with a waymark post to reassure you. Views open to the left, and ahead is a clearly defined route snaking uphill, the last climb on this section before Felindre.

Installing one of the fine wooden Glyndŵr's Way waymark posts on Beacon Hill.

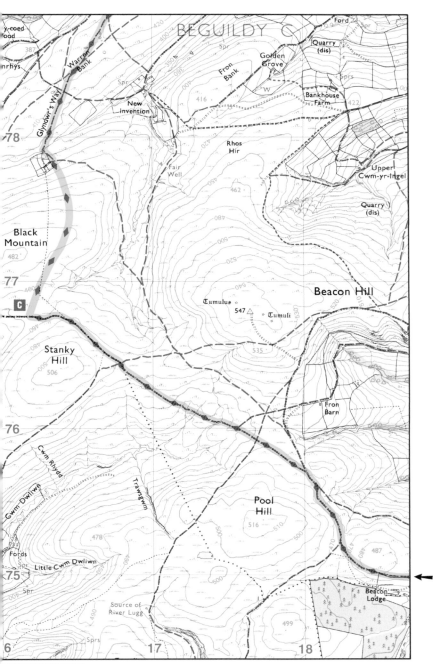

BEGUILDY C

Ford

Quarry
(dis)

Golden
Grove

Fron
Bank

Bankhouse
Farm

New
Invention

Rhos
Hir

Upper
Cwm-yr-Ingel

Fair
Well

Quarry
(dis)

Black
Mountain

Beacon Hill

Tumulus

547

Tumuli

Stanky
Hill

Fron
Barn

Cwm Rhydd

Trawsgwm

Pool
Hill

Cwm Dwliwn

Fords

Little Cwm Dwliwn

Source of
River Lugg

Beacon
Lodge

ntours are given in metres
he vertical interval is 10m

Looking south-east from Stanky Hill towards Beacon Hill Common on a fine open stretch of high ground.

At a track junction continue ahead to cross a gate and a stile and carry on ahead up Cefn Pawl, soon climbing a stony track that veers to the right. A lonely waymark post appears. The track then meets a road **D**, which you cross, and then veer half-left to a fence corner. Bear to the right, keeping the fence to your right. When you reach a gate, go through it and follow the track to the right. Very shortly you reach a second gate on the right. At this point you veer off to the left by a waymark post, to head towards a second post and enjoy the very fine wide views across valley to the right. Carry on along a faint track as directed by a waymark post. In the bottom corner of a bracken-covered field you reach a stile by a gate. Cross this and carry on with a fence to the left. Cross another stile beside a gate and continue with the fence still on your left. There are good views here over Felindre, and a spectacular view over the valley ahead, bisected by the River Teme, where the hillsides are divided into small fields punctuated by the occasional farmhouse. Cross a stile by a gate and continue down the track, zig-zagging steeply towards Brandy House Farm (B&B). Leaving the house to your right you continue down the track to the road, passing two cattle grids. At the road, you turn left to reach Felindre.

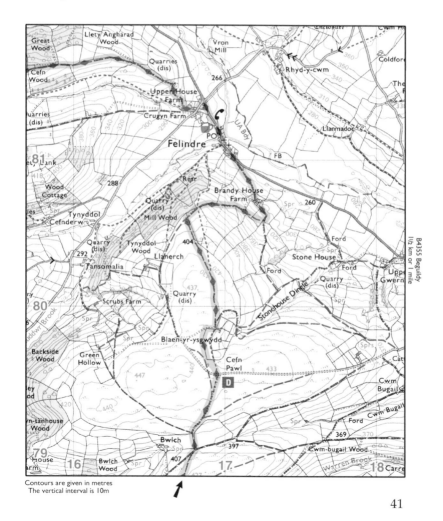

Contours are given in metres
The vertical interval is 10m

The Heart of Wales Line

The railway line which you pass under just after setting off from Llangunllo runs between Shrewsbury and Swansea, and had its origins in the Llanelly Railway Company, incorporated on 19 June 1828, which built a horse-drawn tramway 2 miles (3.25 km) long between Llanelli Docks and the Gelly Gille coal mine. Track was then laid to Pontarddulais to transport the anthracite which was being mined in the Amnan Valley, and the company obtained two steam engines. Gradually the line extended north, reaching Llandeilo in 1857 and Llandovery in 1858.

To the north, in England, the Shrewsbury & Hereford Railway had built a line to Craven Arms and Stokesay in 1851, and this engendered enthusiasm for a through route to Swansea, with the project being promoted modestly as part of 'one direct and unbroken line of traffic from the German Ocean [the North Sea] to the Atlantic'. By 1860 the line was open as far as Bucknell: in the next year it reached Knighton, finally arriving in Llandrindod Wells in 1865. This was celebrated with the journey of an 18-carriage two-engined train to the town, which brought along with it the band of the Radnorshire Rifle Volunteers, who played during the journey.

The Central Wales Extension Railway was then extended a further 26 miles (41 km) to Llandovery in 1868, thus completing the line. The official opening ceremonies were held in the town with military parades and music, and a celebratory dinner attended by officials of the London & North Western Railway, who had made a substantial loan to help finance the completion of this final section.

After 1948, when the railways were nationalised, the line became part of the Western Region of British Railways. In 1962 BR made an application to close the line, with the immediate result that a committee was formed to save it, chaired by Alderman Tudor Watkins MP. The line survived but was once more threatened in 1967; happily, closure was again avoided and the line's social function was recognised, resulting in a government grant of £370,000 for each of two years.

However, economies on track maintenance meant that by the end of 1980 excursion trains pulled by heavy locomotives could no longer use the line, resulting in the loss of valuable visitor income to Llandrindod and Llanwyrtyd Wells. In 1981 HoWLTA, the Heart of Wales Line Travellers Association, was formed to promote the interests of the railway, and continues to pursue this end energetically.

The Heart of Wales Line Railway, which links Shrewsbury with Swansea, and provides a stunning ride through the centre of Wales.

3 Felindre to Llanbadarn Fynydd
Felindre i Lanbadarn Fynydd

7 ¹/₂ miles (12 km)

There is a post office and stores, and The Wharf Inn (now sadly closed), on your left, in Felindre. You pass these to reach a cross-roads **A**, where you turn left by a large wooden shed/barn. Walk along the lane for about 80 yards and then turn right through a gate to walk across a yard. Go through gates, pass the farmhouse and turn right to leave the yard through another gate. Follow the clear track uphill to a gate, ignoring a gateway to your right, off the track. Continue ahead along a track, at first stony, then grassed, which is incised in the field on the apex of the hill-slope, with expansive views all around.

Go through a gate and continue uphill, with just a few straggly trees to your right. The old hedgerow comes and goes as you continue to climb, finally passing a plantation of

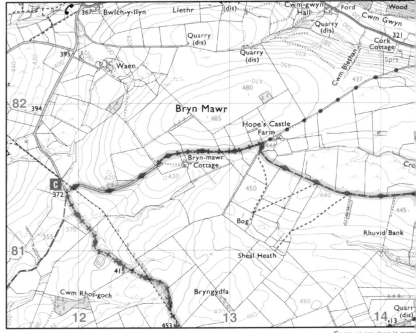

Contours are given in metr
The vertical interval is 10n

conifers. In time, the fine view to the north here will be closed off as the trees grow. Cross a stile beside a gate as you approach the Great Wood, which is just over the fence to your right.

Having left the wood behind, the track becomes more clearly defined, and soon you pass through a gate and continue downhill along an enclosed section of track, which bends to the right and approaches Rhuvid. Pass by the house **B,** using two gates, and immediately begin climbing a stony track. Go through a gate and continue, passing a small conifer plantation on the left. Go through another gate and shortly pass more ragged conifers on the left before you go through a third gate. Continue on through a series of gates to reach a track junction, where you turn right.

Soon the track becomes a surfaced lane, and you turn left to follow it, passing through a gate and continuing along it. In the valley to the left a stream has been dammed to form three ponds, and there are more ponds beside Bryn-mawr cottage. Continue along the road and, just before a steep dip, turn left **C**, passing a cattle grid, and carry on along a clear track.

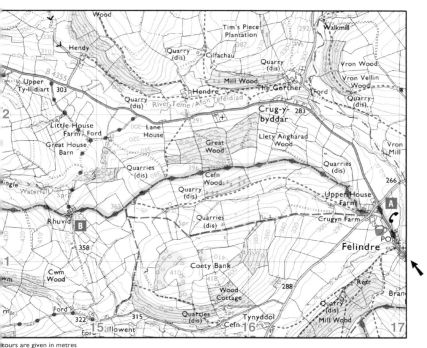

tours are given in metres
vertical interval is 10m

45

When this track bends to the right, go straight ahead through a gate, immediately crossing a stream and continuing ahead over a field to reach a gate. Go through and follow the track uphill and to the right. You pass a tree-fringed pond on your right and carry on climbing, with a valley to your left, to a gate. Go through this and continue uphill, bearing left to reach another gate. Go through and enter an old plantation. Follow the track and soon leave the wood through a gate to veer right over the brow of the hill ahead, heading for a conspicuous waymark post. Carry on ahead to a gate, which you go through, bearing slightly right to the track which runs over the right-hand side of the hill ahead, passing another waymark post. Cross a farm track and carry on uphill.

When a fence appears on your left, fork right off the main track onto a green track, by a waymark post. On the top of the hill to your right is Castell-y-blaidd (castle of the wolf) **5**. There is a wonderful view from the summit, but unfortunately no right-of-way to give you access. This is the site of an unfinished 13th-century castle, which was probably abandoned for the better situation of Tinboeth, about 4 miles (6.5 km) to the south-west. Go through a gate **D** and walk to a waymark post ahead, passing a marshy patch. Veer right to a stile by a gate beside a livestock pen. Cross it and join the road, where you turn right.

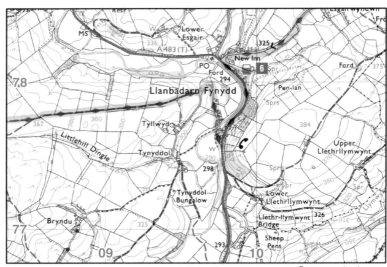

Contours are given in metres
The vertical interval is 10m

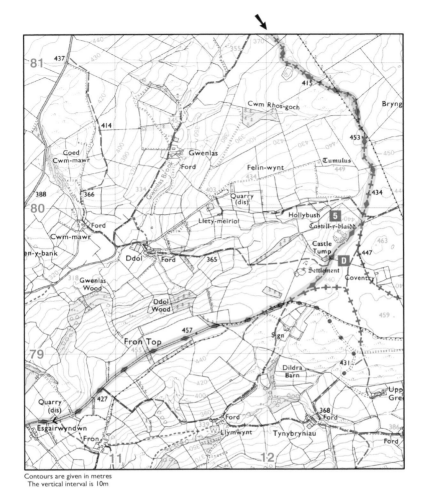

Contours are given in metres
The vertical interval is 10m

Go through a gate and continue, enjoying the fine view ahead. Soon you'll notice the tall turbines of a wind farm on the horizon to your right. Pass a few straggly trees at Fron Top before descending towards Llanbadarn Fynydd. A short way beyond the new farmhouse at Esgairwyndwn look out for a stile on the left. Cross this and continue downhill, with a hedge on your right, then bear to the left to go through a gateway. Now walk to the right, parallel to a fence. Ignore the cattle grid on your right and continue down to a stile. Cross this and carry on down to Llanbadarn Fynydd, where you turn left. Pass a memorial stone to reach The New Inn **6**, which serves real ale and meals, has a nice garden and welcomes children.

4 Llanbadarn Fynydd to Abbeycwmhir
Llanbadarn Fynydd i Abaty Cwm Hir

8 ¹/₄ miles (13 km)

Walk along the pavement at Llanbadarn Fynydd, with The New Inn to your left. Carefully cross the road, and maintain your direction, now beside the Afon Ieithon, a trout stream. Pass a church below you to the right and then turn right **A** to follow a road which bends to the right. Cross the bridge and continue, passing some houses and then following a hairpin bend to the left. About 25 yards after the bend, turn right, but not sharp right, along a track.

Now you start gently climbing. Go through a gate ahead and carry on with a fence on your left, passing through another gate and continuing to a stile beside a gate, before trees. Cross this and turn left **B**, to walk with a fence on your left. Cross a stile beside a gate and walk ahead, over an open common, veering left and looking for a waymark post amongst the gorse. When you have located it, follow the faint track as indicated. The marshy hollows of this route guide you through a wide boggy patch, where a boardwalk helps to keep your feet dry, but the worst of the mud is eventually left behind as the track becomes clearer. Now you are walking along the side of a gloriously lonely valley.

As the track descends, the views widen, with the Brecon Beacons and the Black Mountains on the far horizon. You pass a plantation on your left, which is framed by a lovely overgrown stone wall. Cross a track, which enters forestry land, and carry on ahead by a bank, keeping the fence to your left. Be sure to ignore a track which forks away uphill to your right. Walking beside another fine rough stone wall on the left you suddenly notice the noise of traffic, a sound unheard for several miles. Continue your descent, following a sunken path and with conifers to the left.

A fence joins from the left and eventually you reach a gate beside a house. Go through and continue downhill. Go through a gate near a small corrugated iron barn and continue. Go through another gate and carry on, following the track as it bends right through a gate into Tynypant farmyard. You now turn left to pass through a gateway **C** onto the road. On a nearby summit to the north-east, just across the Afon Ieithon, is Tinboeth **7**, which may have been Roger Mortimer's Castle dating from 1282, and known as 'Dynbaud'. It stood until 1322, when it was surrendered to the

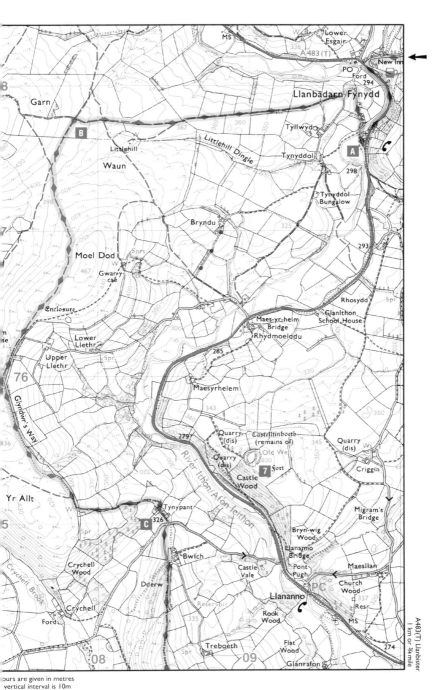

MS
Lower Esgair
A 483 (T)
New Inn
Garn
PO
Ford 294
Llanbadarn Fynydd
B
Littlehill
Tyllwyd
Littlehill Dingle
Waun
Tynyddol
A
298
Tynyddol Bungalow
Bryndu
Moel Dod
293
Gwarry-cae
Rhosydd
Enclosure
Glanithon School House
Maes-yr-helm Bridge
Lower Llethr
Rhydmoelddu
285
Upper Llethr
76
Maesyrhelem
Glyndwr's Way
343
279
Quarry (dis)
Castelltinboeth (remains of)
Quarry (dis)
Old Well
350
Quarry (dis)
Fort
7
Criggin
River Ithon/Afon Ieithon
Castle Wood
Yr Allt
Migram's Bridge
Tynypant
C 326
Bryn-wig Wood
Llanamo Bridge
Crychell Wood
Bwlch
Castle Vale
Pont-Pugh
PC
Maesllan
Dderw
Church Wood
Resr
Crychell
Reservoir
Llananno
Ford
Rook Wood
MS
Treboeth
Flat Wood
Glanrafon
274

A483(T) Llanbister
1 km or ¾ mile

ours are given in metres
vertical interval is 10m

49

The view south-west from Ysgwd-ffordd, about halfway between Llanbadarn Fynydd and Abbeycwmhir.

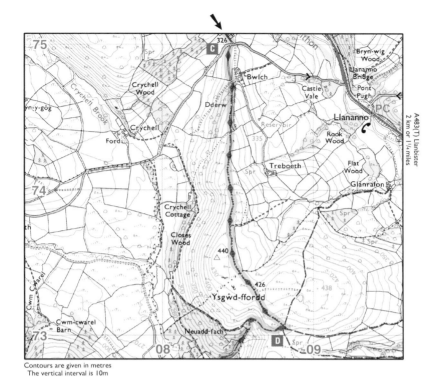

Contours are given in metres
The vertical interval is 10m

King following the conquest of Wales. It then fell into ruin and little remains to be seen, apart from traces of the gatehouse.

Carefully cross the road and walk up the lane opposite, towards Bwlch Farm. Just before reaching the farm turn right through a gate and continue steeply uphill, with conifers to your left. When the trees are passed, go through the gate ahead and continue, with a fence on your left. There are excellent views to both left and right as you climb. Carry on ahead as the fence curves away on your left, looking for a waymark post on the nearest hill ahead. Walk towards it, but as you do so don't forget to look back and enjoy the view. Carry on ahead, passing an Ordnance Survey trig. point on the summit to the right and a waymark post, which directs you to ignore a track off to the left.

When the path descends to a dip between summits, turn sharp right at a waymark post **D** and follow the route down off the mountain. Note the dark conifer plantation ahead – your path descends and then goes right through them. So, turn left at the waymark post, walking down the cwm to cross a stile by a gate on the right, and enter the trees. Follow the very pleasant

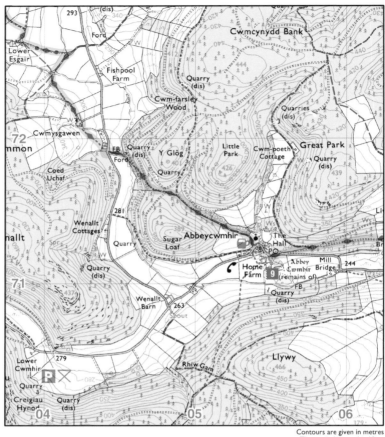

Contours are given in metres
The vertical interval is 10m

path downhill, which winds its way through fine mixed woodland, and later conifers. Leave the forest through a gate and go
down to another gate that leads onto a driveway. Continue
walking downhill to a bridle gate on the right, from where the
path leads you round to a footbridge; after crossing this you
follow the driveway uphill to a lane **E**. Turn left and walk along
the lane for approximately $1^1/_4$ mile (2 km). Ignore a stile up on
a bank to your right and continue, descending to Dyfaenor **8**, a
mansion built by the Fowler family, its owners during the Civil
War, and then immediately fork up the track to the right **F**. Go
through a wooden gate and continue uphill when the path
forks, soon walking with a fence to your right. Ignore a stile on
your right and continue ahead.

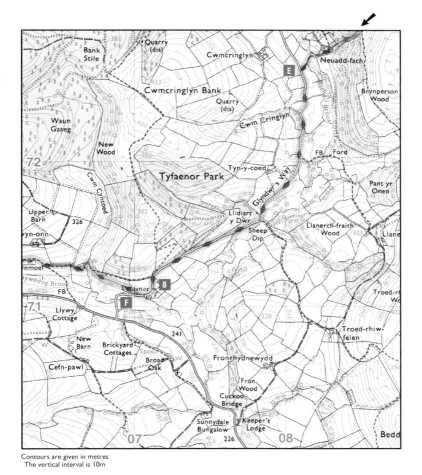

Contours are given in metres
The vertical interval is 10m

Cross a footbridge and then climb up the slope to a stile. Cross this and carry on, keeping the fence to your right. Cross a stile on the right to walk behind Brynmoil, keeping the fence to your left.

Descend, go through a gate, and carry on along a track. This soon becomes a road, and you maintain your direction as you join the main road to reach Abbeycwmhir. You pass the ruined abbey **9** on your left before reaching the church and The Happy Union Inn. This village pub looks very enticing, but don't count on getting refreshment here until after 9.00pm or so, and not on Sundays. It keeps very late weekday hours! Whether it is open or not, look out for the fascinating old sign fixed to its side wall.

Abbeycwmhir

Abbeycwmhir has a fascination which belies its present size. In the 12th century it was chosen as the site for an ambitious, but now almost forgotten, abbey which was exceeded in size only by Durham and Winchester. It was built by the Cistercians, for whom this remote site was ideal, as the nearby river satisfied their dietary needs and also enabled them to build a mill. The fish ponds they created still exist, some if only in name: Fishpool Farm lies 1 $1/2$ miles (2.5 km) to the north-west, and Llyn Gwyn, near Nant Glas, is said still to contain fish descended from those stocked by the monks. Their industry also improved the productivity of the surrounding land, and their compassion benefited the local needy.

The original building, founded in 1143, was abandoned, but the abbey was soon re-founded upon its present site in 1176. Annexed by the Mortimer family, and later by King John of England, it was returned to Welsh control in 1227 when Llywelyn Fawr began to build the grand cathedral whose remains can be seen today.

It is not clear whether the abbey ever truly prospered, since it was severely penalised during the war between Llywelyn the Great and Henry III of England. The headless body of Llywelyn was secretly interred in the abbey in 1282, following his execution in London, and you can see a memorial to him amongst the ruins. The abbey continued to support the Welsh Princes, and was consequently starved of funds by the English Crown. It was attacked and burnt by Owain Glyndŵr's army in 1401, as it was under the patronage of the Mortimers, and eventually became Crown property in 1461 before being dissolved, along with the other monasteries, by Henry VIII. The remains were fortified during the Civil War and held by the Royalists until the abbey was finally totally destroyed by cannon under the command of General Fairfax. Stone from the ruined abbey was used to build Dyfaenor, a handsome house passed on Glyndŵr's Way, and the original village church. A large part of the building, consisting of five arches from the arcade, and some roof timbers with their grotesquely carved supports, were re-used when the church in Llanidloes was rebuilt circa 1542.

Descending through Neuadd-fach woods, on the approach to Abbeycwmhir – a pleasant change from the ubiquitous forest plantations seen throughout Mid Wales.

5 Abbeycwmhir to Blaentrinant
Abaty Cwm Hir i Blaentrinant

6 ³/₄ miles (11 km)

From the church in Abbeycwmhir walk to the right, with The
Happy Union Inn to your left, and turn right by the old petrol
pump **A**. As you walk up the lane the church is soon below you
to the right, with water tumbling from an arch on the edge of
the graveyard. When you reach a stile, cross it and continue
along a green track.

You start gently climbing with a stream below you on the
right, and forestry woodland ahead. When you reach a stile
beside a wooden gate, cross it and continue along a sunken
green lane, which continues to climb gently through a tall and
dense forestry plantation. When you reach a waymark post at a
track junction continue ahead. At a forest road cross straight
over and carry on ahead – the track now dips, and you stay on
this, ignoring the forest road. When another forest track crosses
obliquely, continue ahead and downhill. Again, a forest road
makes an oblique crossing, and once again you continue ahead
and downhill. There is now a small stream to your left and,

The church at Abbeycwmhir may have been built using stones from the ruined abbey.

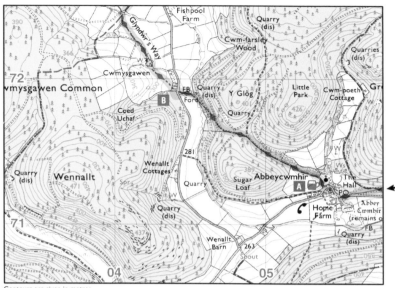

Contours are given in metres
The vertical interval is 10m

beyond that, a road. When the path dips, continue ahead for about 20 yards and then turn left to cross a footbridge. Continue along the track, which in wet weather has a small stream running along it, and soon it becomes a hollow lane brightened with bluebells in spring. It then climbs to join a road **B**.

Turn left and walk along the road for 20 yards, then turn right to continue along a rough track, with a forest plantation to your left and a low corrugated-iron shed to your right. Shortly a stile appears on the right. Cross this and cross the bridge over a tiny stream, then walk ahead skirting the bottom of the hill to your left. Cross another small stream, and walk across a marshy patch, with barns to your left, to reach a stile. Cross this and follow the track, keeping the farmhouse to your left and crossing a stile beside a gate, to continue up the track. You now have a fine view across the valley to your right.

When the track bends to the left, cross a stile over to the right, ignoring a gate and an old gateway. Now veer left, descending across the field towards a gate and a stile. Just before you reach the stile you ford a stream, where there is a weird optical illusion, rather like the famous 'electric brae' in Scotland: the water appears to flow uphill! Cross the stile and then continue ahead along the track. Do not turn left.

At last you are walking over level ground, and there are pretty low hills all around, dotted with isolated farms. When the track joins a lane, turn very sharply left through a gateway, heading towards Lower Esgair. You are now walking on tarmac, and climbing very gently.

Go through a gate by a house and veer right along the track, leaving the house behind. Stay on the track as it bends to the left, ignoring a little stile and a gate to your right. You continue gently climbing and pass a double-fenced hedge on your left, which is being regenerated, and continue on up the hill.

When you reach a gate, go through it and then veer off the track to the right to go through the next gate immediately ahead, and continue with the hedge to your left. Go through another gate and carry on, keeping slightly left with the hedge on your left. As you gently traverse the brow of the hill the views to both right and left are excellent.

Go through a gate in the field corner and turn right, continuing uphill along a farm track towards a gate. Go through this gate and veer half-right uphill towards a gate which is just below the near horizon. Go through this and turn left, to walk with the fence on your left. You are still climbing, so if you need to catch your breath, stop and enjoy the splendid view over the valley, with bare hills to the left and large areas of forest to the right, enlivened with a sprinkling of farmhouses.

Go through the next gate and turn right, keeping the fence to your right, to walk up to a gate. Go through this and carry on, with the fence still to your right. Again you are walking up the brow of a hill, with superb views all around. Go through the first metal gate on your right into a small enclosure and walk across this to a gateway on the opposite side. Go through and carry on, keeping a fence to your left and the very rounded hill summit to your right. The faint profile of the path can be seen as a notch in the hillside ahead, by the fence. When the fence leaves your path, heading off half-left, you continue ahead towards a waymark post. The view on the northern side has now opened up – it is a wide valley with a few scattered trees, framed by distant low hills. You pass a fenced conifer plantation to the right before reaching a rough track by a fence ahead **C**. Here you turn right and at last start walking downhill towards Bwlch-y-sarnau **10**.

At the bottom of the hill you reach a gate with a stile beside it. Cross this stile and continue ahead. When you join a track veer right, walking gently uphill, beside a small bungalow. Soon you join a road and turn left, ignoring the fork in the road to your right. Pass the chapel, the graveyard and the community centre to your right, to turn right down a track by a red telephone kiosk **D**. Go through a wooden gate to the right of the house and carry on ahead along a sunken track, with a fence to your left. Go through the bridle gate ahead and continue, still with the fence to your left. The field is very rough, so just pick your own route down to go through another bridle gate ahead. Follow the path ahead through what was, at the time of writing

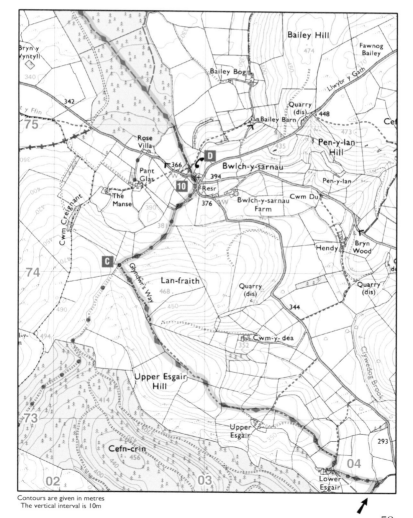

Contours are given in metres
The vertical interval is 10m

(spring 2003), a large expanse of felled trees; waymark posts guide you along the path through tussocky grass and eventually your traverse of this felled forest ends at a forest road, which you join and turn right.

You carry on to cross a bridge over a stream and enter a standing forest, which immediately seems more reassuring and amenable – certainly the walking is much easier and the cool, moist ambience of the trees is pleasantly refreshing. Continue along the main track to reach a gate, through which you leave the forest to join a road E. Turn left and then, after 20 yards, turn right along a minor road, and stay on this as it turns sharply right, and then left, passing cottages at Waun. It is a wide, open landscape here, set in a broad valley enclosed by rounded mountains and speckled with forest plantations under an open sky, all very peaceful and quite remote. The road continues through this panorama and eventually starts to climb gently. As you reach the summit the road veers left – but you fork off right along a forest road and continue climbing, with trees to your right. This is a popular practice area for the local off-road motorcyclists, whom you may meet on the track. Don't worry – you will hear them coming, and most will respond favourably to a friendly wave. There are fine views to the north-west, with a wind farm on the horizon. When a track joins from the left you continue ahead. As the plantation ends you reach a metal gate – go through and continue along the clear track to reach Trinnant.

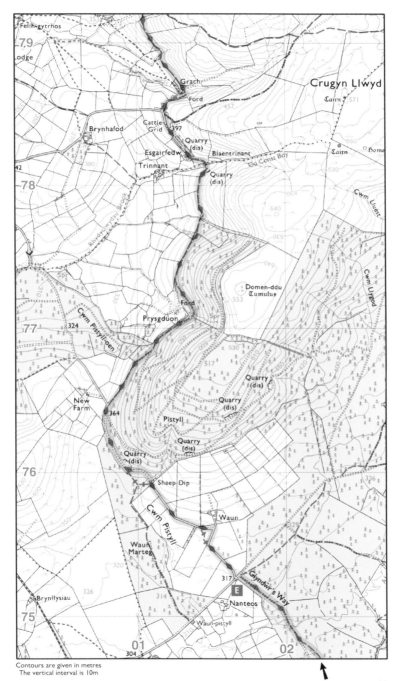

Contours are given in metres
The vertical interval is 10m

61

6 Blaentrinant to Llanidloes
Blaentrinant i Lanidloes

8 ¹/₂ miles (13.5 km)

By the entrance to Trinnant Farm you reach a wooden gate and a stile. Cross this and continue ahead (do not go down the lane to the house). The track becomes a road at Esgairfedw **A** and you continue, walking slightly uphill. Stay on the road when a track leaves to the right. When the road bends to the left and starts to descend, and a track joins from the right from behind trees, you continue straight ahead as directed by the waymark post up to the right. Go through a gate into the farmyard at Grach and carry on, passing barns to the left. You continue, descending to a stream and crossing a footbridge just below a little waterfall and reaching a stile beside a gate. Cross this and continue ahead and slightly right up to another stile by a waymark post, and cross this as well.

Carry on ahead, walking above Rhiw-felin and soon with the tumbled remains of an old wall on your left. You join a track by a wooden bridleway signpost and turn left. Go downhill and through a gate, and continue downhill along the track. The surface becomes tarmac when a track joins from the left. Continue

The descent to Cwm from Ffrwd Fawr.

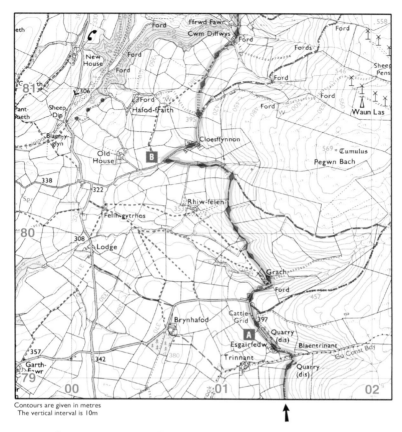

Contours are given in metres
The vertical interval is 10m

and, when you join another road **B**, turn very sharply right by a fine sign for Cloesffynnon, painted on an old mangle. Go through the gate by the house and continue along the road, climbing steadily. As you near the summit of this hill take the track off to the left, walk ahead for 20 yards and then turn right. Follow the track past a cattle grid beside a gate and continue walking beneath the wind farm, up to your right. The views are now becoming a little more dramatic, the hills are a little more pronounced, and the horizon promises some challenging summits.

Go through a gate by buildings and continue along the track, passing through another gate and veering left with the track, and then down to a ford, which you cross and continue, passing through a gate and climbing the track. Having passed a ruined cottage, the next one on the left, Ffrwd Fawr, has been tastefully restored.

The Llandinam wind farm on the Pegwn ridge above Llidiart-y-waun. You will pass more of these structures, with time to decide whether you are for or against.

The path continues climbing up to a gate, which you go through, and then veer left down to a second gate, which you also go through, to follow the track, initially steeply downhill and then less so. Go through a gate and follow the track, which bends to the right. The hillside to your left is covered with a fine variety of deciduous trees, with the wind farm **11** dominating the tops to your right. You now start to descend amidst a very pretty landscape, and soon the sound of tumbling water emanates from a cwm on the right.

You zig-zag down to the valley bottom and approach a stream. Do not cross the stream but turn sharp left to walk along the track, with the water to your right. The track then fords the stream, but walkers can use the footbridge thoughtfully provided. Ignore the first gate on your right and continue uphill as the track becomes rougher. Soon a waymark post directs you to cross a stile to your right.

Now walk half-left up the field to a stile before woods. The approach is very steep, so stop now and again to catch your breath and enjoy the view. Cross the stile and turn left, following the track and going through a gate. The track continues its steady climb amongst deciduous trees. Some compensation for the severity of the climb is provided by a splendid view to the left, clear hilltops above forest, with the odd isolated farm. Eventually you reach a road and turn right **C**, to continue climbing. The full expanse of the wind farm is now visible on the summits to your right. Eventually the road peters out as you approach a cattle grid. Go past this, ignore the fork on your right to Penybanc and continue ahead and slightly uphill. Eventually you cross the summit of the hill, and an absolutely splendid view opens ahead over the valley of the River Severn.

Cross a stile by a gate and walk through a small field, with a fence to your right. Go through another gate and continue ahead, ignoring a gate to your right, but keeping the fence to your right. When you reach a waymark post, with a gate to the right of it **D**, turn sharply left. You will immediately see another waymark which enables you pick up a clear track with a fence to the right. Continue ahead, ignoring a gate off to the right. Ignore another gate just before a house on the right, but veer slightly left and walk beside Moelfre, an attractive house.

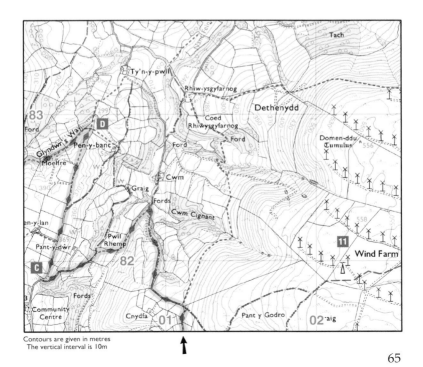

Contours are given in metres
The vertical interval is 10m

The track then descends to go through a gate. Cross a stream, swing to the right and then veer left uphill towards a waymark post, to follow the path. Keep bearing to the left and gradually climbing around the hill. When you reach a gate, go through and continue ahead, keeping just to the left of some trees. You cross a stream and find you are now walking along a clear track which gently descends to join another track. Veer left and continue uphill. As the track nears the summit, do not go through the gate ahead, but instead go off the track to the right, through a gate and turn sharp left, crossing a stile and walking with a fence to your left. When you reach a gate on your left, where a green track crosses your route, follow the waymark post ahead and just slightly to the right. You cross rough pasture and, as you reach the brow of the hill, you will see a stile ahead of you.

Cross this and turn sharp right to walk with a fence on your right. Go through a gate and continue ahead to a second gate, which you also go through and then turn sharply left to walk to a stile. Cross this and walk half-right across the field. As you cross the brow you will see a waymark post ahead. When you reach it turn right and walk to a track, where you turn left downhill. Ignore the track which leaves to your left over a cattle grid, going instead through the gate ahead and walk on, with a ditch and a fence on your left. Go through a gate and continue ahead with the fence to your left. As you reach the bottom of the field look for a waymark post. Turn right here and walk with the old banked hedge to your right. You then descend quite steeply as a fence joins from the right. You are now walking above a lovely tree-lined cwm. You descend to a stream, cross the bridge and stiles and turn right, to follow the path uphill in a wooded glade. Keep climbing steeply, ignoring little paths which branch off to the right and then, after climbing a steep slope, you arrive at a waymark post which directs you to walk to the left, climbing the field with the hedge and the fence on your right. Continue through a gap in an old hedge and then go through a gate to join a road **E**, where you turn right. When you reach a T-junction, turn right and continue. You descend to a road junction, with a magnificent view ahead, and turn left. You then pass the pretty Chapel Baptist Church **12** to the right: this was founded in 1740, rebuilt in 1850, restored in 1905, destroyed by fire in 1954 and finally (we hope!) rebuilt in 1957.

The lane passes a new red-brick house on the left and then, when it bends to the right, you veer off left and walk down a field, with a hedge on your left, to reach a stile, which you cross

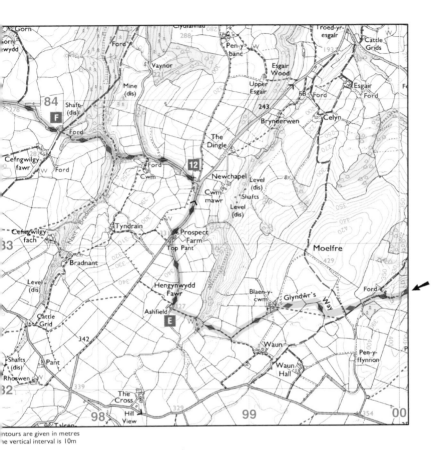

ntours are given in metres
ie vertical interval is 10m

and then turn right. You then turn sharp left at a waymark post
to zig-zag downhill towards the stream. Look out for a stile on
your right and cross it, and then immediately cross the bridge
and stile. Don't turn sharp right as you come off the bridge, but
walk uphill and follow the path half-right as directed by the
waymark post. As you climb you join another path: just keep
swinging to the left as you climb uphill. The path then curves
around to the right and continues climbing. When a hedge
joins from the left continue straight on along a clear path,
ignoring a gate to your left. When the path splits, ignore the
green path to your left and continue ahead, crossing a tiny
stream and bearing to the right up the hill to a gateway.

Go through the gateway and continue up the field to a stile **F**.
Cross it and continue walking ahead along the road. Although

The Clywedog Dam, a vast edifice which towers over the more picturesque remains of the Bryntail Mine.

the approach to Llanidloes is by road, it is quite a quiet and pleasant one – progressing down a valley with a stream on your left, with an occasional block of conifers to break up the grassland beneath the surrounding low peaks. The views ahead are good. The lane continues its descent and gradually the first signs of Llanidloes appear. Shortly after the road turns sharply to the left, turn right between houses to join a path which crosses the bypass via a modern footbridge. You pass the handsome railway station building **13** on the right. This was built in 1864 and was the head office of, in turn, the Manchester & Milford Railway, Cambrian Railways and the Great Western Railway until the line finally closed in 1962. You then pass the fire station and continue ahead along Cambrian Place, which joins Great Oak Street, passing the imposing Town Hall **14** on the right. This building in the Classic Renaissance style was erected in 1908 as a gift to the Borough from the Davies family of Plasdinam. Walk ahead to the handsome Market Hall, the only surviving example of a half-timbered market hall in Wales.

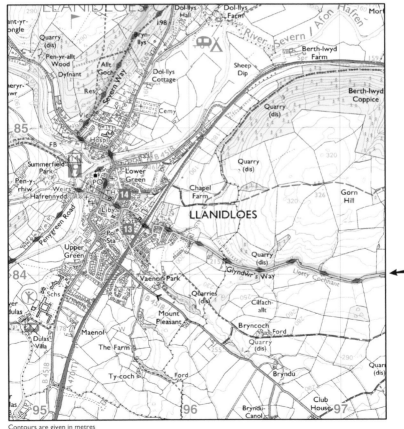

Contours are given in metres
The vertical interval is 10m

69

Llanidloes Market Hall and the Rebecca Riots

This handsome building dates from circa 1600 and is built in 'post and pan' style on the site of the old market cross. It is supported on wooden posts, with a south wall built of stone and a north wall built of brick and dating from 1763. The pretty rooftop cupola houses a curfew bell. John Wesley (1703–91) preached here – you can see his 'pulpit stone' in the north-west corner – and during the 18th century yearly meetings were held here by the Quakers, although episcopal reports revealed that even though 'pockets of Friends (Quakers) were still to be found at Esgair-goch, Trefeglwys,

Llanidloes very handsome Market Hall: Wesley's preaching stone will be found on the

Llanidloes, Llanwddyn and Meifod, the signs of spiritual ebb and apathy are plain to see'.

The Chartists held a meeting here before their unsuccessful 1839 'Rebecca Riot', part of a series of protests against the high tolls that had to be paid on the turnpike roads. These disturbances took their name either from a lady called Rebecca who lent clothes to Twm Carnabwth, the leader of the protest, to disguise himself when making attacks on property, or, as is more commonly suggested, from the Biblical character: 'And they blessed Rebecca, and said unto her, Thou art our sister. Be thou the mother of thousands of millions, and let thy seed possess the gates of those that hate them'. Take your pick!

...it-hand corner. You can have a rest and chat to the locals on the seat.

7 Llanidloes to Afon Biga
Llanidloes i Afon Biga

9 miles (14.5 km)

From the Market Hall walk along Long Bridge Street, passing several pubs, Hamers butchers (by appointment to past royalty: look for the coat of arms), and St Idloes' Church **15** tucked away behind buildings to the left of Picton Street. This church is a very handsome, squat and sturdy building, with a massive 14th-century stone tower topped by a 'Montgomeryshire' belfry. Be sure to go inside to see the five arches of the rebuilt 13th-century arcade, which was taken from Abbeycwmhir around 1542, standing beneath a very fine hammerbeam roof which is decorated with shields and carved angels. The church stands on the site of the original settlement, located at the point where an ancient trackway forded the Rivers Severn and Clwyedog. The remainder of the town dates from the late 13th century, when Edward I granted a market charter to Lord Owain de la Pole of Arwystli.

Continuing along Long Bridge Street you pass a useful Spar grocery on the right before reaching a small roundabout **A**. Here you turn left to cross the bridge, passing Somerfield Park, which overlooks Severn Porte, the confluence of the rivers Severn and Clywedog. Now take the first turning on the left, to walk along Westgate Street, passing a pretty Victorian terrace as the road begins to climb. Pass Tan yr Allt, the last cul de sac to your right and, just beyond this, turn right to walk along a path above bungalows to your right, with rhododendrons to your left.

The path climbs steadily, giving a pleasant view over Llanidloes. When you reach a kissing-gate, go through and continue. You are now entering Allt Goch **16**. The woodlands are now owned and managed by Llanidloes Town Council, having been acquired in 1936 from the Morris-Eyton family. There is a rich variety of trees here, including oak, sycamore, beech, birch, rowan, holly, hazel, Scots pine and Douglas fir.

The path continues climbing, and waymarks indicate that you are now sharing your route with the Severn Way **17**, the longest riverside walk in Britain, stretching fully 210 miles (338 km) from source to sea. Carry on ahead when a track joins from the left, and eventually the route levels out and you continue straight on, passing a picnic area. Ignore a path which leaves to

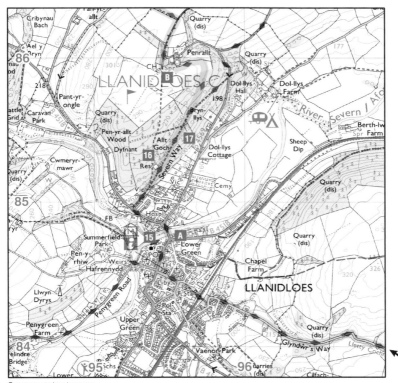

Contours are given in metres
The vertical interval is 10m

the right and continue ahead along the track for about 100 yards, then fork left, up through the woods as directed by a waymark post. Take care to maintain your direction through the woodland and look out for the waymark posts which beckon you ahead, climbing all the while. Go through a gap in the fence and carry straight on, looking out for the next waymark post to guide you, which signals a slight change of direction, to the left, as you begin to descend. Look for a further waymark post beyond a tree, where you turn left to walk with a fence to your right. Just before corrugated-iron farm buildings on your right a waymark post confirms you are still walking in the correct direction.

You emerge from the trees and scrubland onto the edge of a golf course and, before you reach the St Idloes Golf Club clubhouse, you turn right **B** through a gap in the fence as waymarked to walk along a tarmac road. When a lane joins from the left, before a black-and-white timbered house, turn left. You pass farm sheds and continue ahead through a gateway, ignoring a lane and another gateway to the left and another gate into the field to the right. Then, by the next gateway on the left, turn left to pass through and walk with the hedge to your left. At last views of the uplands to the north-west become apparent. Go through a gateway and continue ahead, with a fine view over the Fan. Cross a stile and veer half-right, descending a field to reach a gate in the corner, which you go through to join a road and turn right.

Follow the road for a short way as it bends to the left downhill, and then turn off left as the road bears to the right. Don't enter the farmyard, but take the stile in front of you. Now walk down to a stile, keeping the fence to your left. Cross this stile and continue ahead with the hedge still to your left and Van directly ahead. Pass through a gap in the hedge and continue, crossing the brow and dropping steeply downhill to a stile. Cross this and continue, still with the hedge to your left to walk down to a gate, which you go through. Cross the road and walk ahead along the lane directly opposite. Shortly after the lane bends to the left, look for a waymark post by a large tree on the right, and walk, as directed, uphill across rough ground, rich with bluebells in the spring, to reach a stile, which you cross and then continue along a track, with a hedge to your right. Pass a stand of mature Scots pines and continue along the track as it bends round to the left. Below you to the right are the disused workings of the Van mine, and soon the Van pool appears.

The Van mine **18** was once the most productive lead mine in Britain and, in its heyday, brought great prosperity to Llanidloes. The search for the lode began in 1850, and was initially unsuccessful. Captain Williams started looking again in 1854 and, having spent just five shillings, discovered the lode. Extraction began on a very small scale and continued until 1865, when a rich lode was discovered 180 feet (55 metres) beneath the surface. A 50- x 4-foot (15- x 1.2-metre) waterwheel, the Mary Emma, was built to drive the crusher, and in 1868 the mine was sold for £46,000. Soon an experienced observer commented that the mine contained 'one of the finest and richest lodes I ever saw', and shares began rapidly to increase in value, with the mine soon being valued at over £1 million. Its prosperity was such that a branch of the mainline railway was laid from Caersws, initially to carry freight and, later, passengers. In 1870 the mine yielded an unprecedented 4,370 tons of ore, almost twice as much as its great rival Dylife, which is passed later on Glyndŵr's Way. By 1876 over 700 men were employed, and a 70-inch (178-cm) Cornish pumping engine was installed. Further unexpected discoveries of ore prolonged the life of the mine, but closure finally came in 1921, by which time its cumulative output totalled 96,739 tons of lead ore and 28,424 tons of blende (the common ore of zinc).

Go through a gate and follow the track uphill towards a way-mark post beyond the old mine workings, which are still visible on the hillside. As the clear track that you are following bends left to pass to the left of the summit of the hill, you carry on straight ahead along a fainter green track. Pass the summit of Garth Hill to your left and continue on to a gate. Go through this and follow a fenced and tree-lined green lane. Go through the gate at the end of this fenced section and turn left to walk down a small field, with a drainage ditch and the remnants of a hedgerow to your right, towards a waymark post. After crossing a marshy patch you reach a fence, where you turn right to walk across rough pasture, with the fence and another drainage ditch to your left. When you reach the field corner, cross a railway-sleeper bridge over the ditch, then cross the stile and carry on ahead, with the fence still to your left. Go through a small gate and continue ahead, gently climbing with the fence and the hedge still to your left. Pen y banc Farm is over to your right. Just before you reach a wide metal gate in the field corner, turn sharp left to cross a stile, then turn sharp right to walk with the fence, and a lane, to your right. Cross the stile ahead, walk up to the road **C** and turn right, watching out for traffic.

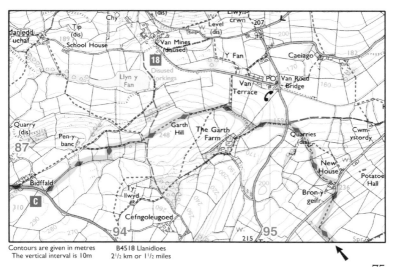

Contours are given in metres   B4518 Llanidloes
The vertical interval is 10m   2½ km or 1½ miles

Fortunately there is a green verge where you can take refuge as necessary. Pass the road-sign to Llyn Clywedog and the lead mine and carry on along the main road. As you labour up the hill you can enjoy a final fine view of the Van pool, over to your right.

The road levels out and then dips slightly before climbing again: look for the track to your left and branch off the road along this, passing a cattle grid. Soon a fine view of the Clywedog Valley opens. Approaching Bryntail Farm **19** you pass a pond to your left. Several thousand tons of lead ore was extracted from shallow workings around here in the 1930s by Isaac Jones. Go through the gate ahead, then enter the farmyard through a gate. Go through another two gates and pass through a farmyard with some very fine old farm machinery, then cross a stile to leave. Continue along the clear track, passing more old buildings and abandoned mine-workings to your left. Cross a stile by a gate and soon the track begins its descent into the valley. Abandoned mine workings now become more prominent. Ignore a gate to your right as the Clywedog Dam comes into view, and continue on down the track, which curves to the right. Go through a small gate and continue. The track swings down the hill towards the dam, overlooked by the rather boxy and functional control-room on the far side. As you follow the path down through woodland, the remains of the Bryntail mine buildings appear below you and to the right. When you have finished the descent, you may like to explore the remains of the old lead mine.

The Bryntail Mine **20** is a very ancient enterprise which exploits the eastern end of the Van lode. It is recorded as being worked in 1708, but then fell into disuse until a revival during the early 1800s, when a 25- x 5-foot (7.6- x 1.5-metre) waterwheel was installed, having been transported by a coaster from Cornwall to Aberystwyth. The mine's most productive year was 1851, when 384 tons of lead ore were extracted, but from then on losses gradually accumulated, in spite of changes of ownership and management. A very fine 60-foot (18.25-metre) waterwheel was installed in 1870, using a 6-inch (15-cm) rope to pump one of the shafts. The company acquired an adjacent mine in 1870, and new shafts were sunk – all to no avail. A new firm, the New Van Consols & Glyn Company, was formed in 1882, and further shafts were sunk, but the whole venture finally collapsed in 1884.

Cross the wooden footbridge over waterfalls and turn sharp right, keeping the Afon Clywedog to your right. Now follow the

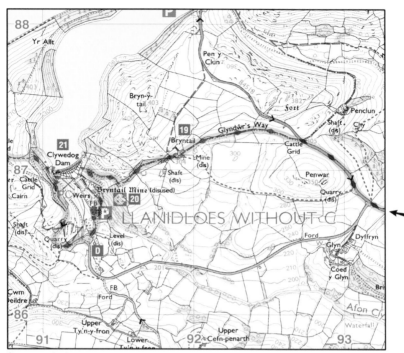

Contours are given in metres
The vertical interval is 10m

track as it bends left uphill and away from the dam. When you reach a road **D** veer right uphill, with houses to your left. At the top of the hill turn right, to walk along a road, initially following the sign which directs you to the Lakeside Drive and Picnic Site. As you approach the summit of this steep hill the road forks: take the right fork. Pass very handsome toilets and a balcony on your left, with splendid views over the dam and the lead mine to your right. Clywedog Dam **21** is a round-headed mass concrete buttress dam: when completed in 1967 it was the tallest in the British Isles. It regulates the flow of water in the River Severn and is 235 feet (72 metres) tall and 752 feet (229 metres) long, with a maximum depth of water of 212 feet (65 metres). A massive 11,000,000,000 gallons of water is impounded; the reservoir covers 615 acres (250 hectares) and is 6 miles (9.5 km) long. Work began on 6 April 1964 and ended on the 22 December 1966.

As the road beside the reservoir makes a sharp hairpin turn to the left, you cross a stile on your right, and begin climbing, with the remains of an old wall to your right. Head towards the waymark post on the horizon ahead and, when you reach it, veer slightly right towards a signpost, with the road just to your left. When you reach the road, turn right, passing a cattle grid, and continue straight on.

The road bends to the left and starts to descend. You pass a pretty and ornate hedge and turn right where signed 'To the Nature Trail'. Go through a little wooden gate beside a larger gate, then turn left to walk by the house and reach a stile, which you cross. There is a very fine view of Llyn Clywedog ahead. Continue with a fence and a hedge to your left. Go through a small wooden gate and walk down a fenced path. Go through another wooden gate and descend steps towards the reservoir. Turn left above the water, to continue walking with the water to your right. Cross a little inlet stream and continue along a narrow, undulating path above the water. Cross a footbridge at the head of an inlet, walk ahead for about 20 yards and then turn right to walk along a narrow path with the water still to your right. The sound of halyards slapping against masts (in season) announces that you are approaching the Clywedog Yacht Club **22**. Climb up through a small stand of trees, ignoring a stile to your left and proceed ahead through a kissing-gate. Take the track ahead and to the left (not down to the water's edge) to pass the sailing club. On summer weekends there is plenty of activity here, with an assortment of craft: yachts, dinghies and sailboards, plus a lively café where the sailors gather to discuss their water-borne exploits.

Pass a cattle grid and then, about 50 yards up the hill, veer off the road to the right to reach a stile. Climb this and turn left to walk with the fence to your left and Clywedog to your right. Step over a small stream and continue. Now, having passed the end of a little inlet, you veer away from the water, walking uphill and tending to the left through trees, following a faint path up to a stile.

Cross this and veer to the left of the trees ahead, looking for a waymark post. When you reach two posts in front of the ruins of Foel, walk between them and tend to the right, walking diagonally uphill, with Clywedog to your right, to reach a stile in the field corner. Cross this and continue along a not very distinct path ahead. Continue uphill as directed by the next post as Clywedog again comes into view, and soon you are walking downhill. Carry on ahead at the next post and, as you cross the brow of the hill heading towards a track beside the reservoir, a waymark post **E** directs you to turn left and walk down to the track.

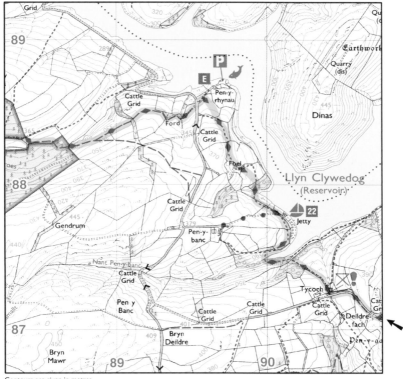

Contours are given in metres
The vertical interval is 10m

Maintain your direction along the track, to walk through a kissing-gate beside a cattle grid. Now cross the road to walk through the gate opposite and continue ahead, following a green track across a field. Pass through a gate, ford a stream and follow the track as it bends right and then left and climbs the hill. The track then swings through an old gateway and continues. There are excellent views to your right across Clywedog as the track contours around the hill and enters a dip, with a row of trees ahead – make for the gap in the trees, where you will reach a waymarked gate. Go through this and continue ahead, initially maintaining your altitude. You will see a waymark post ahead in a gap in another line of trees: pass this and, still maintaining your height and direction, walk to the next post, where the path starts to descend towards a forest plantation. You soon pick your way down to the stream, which you must carefully ford (it can be slippery) and then walk up to a gate to enter the forest.

Follow a clear track through this very dark stand of trees, with a stream initially down to your left. The track eventually bends sharply right and climbs up to a gate. Go through this and turn left, to walk with a fence to your left. When the fence heads away sharply to the left, turn right to walk the short distance across the field and up to a gate. Go through this, turn left and then immediately go through a second gate and continue along the track, beside a stand of young conifers. Soon the track is surrounded by conifers in different stages of development, from the very young to the very old, where gradually, over the coming years, the route will become completely enclosed. However, when this was being written, you could still see a very pretty stream tumbling down a series of gentle falls in the centre of this broad valley.

When the forest track begins to swing around to the west, fork right along a clear, waymarked forest path. Leave the plantation through a gate and walk ahead, crossing rough pasture with a fence over to your left. There are patches of very wet and boggy peat to negotiate as you walk down the field. Gradually veer away from the fence to reach a gate, not far from a small conifer plantation. Go through the gate and follow a rough track downhill, veering to the left. You are now in the midst of a quite bleak and open landscape consisting of rough grazing and marsh, with just conifer plantations to break up the panorama. The only farm in sight is Nant-y-Gwrdu. Go through a gate and continue along the track, but do not go through the next gate. Instead, veer off to the left along the path going downhill. Descend the path to a gateway but again do not go through the gate: instead walk to the left of it and continue with the fence now to your right and a stream on your left. Pass an entrance to some paddocks and carry on with the fence on your right. Pass through a gate to join the road, where you turn left. There is a pleasant picnic site here, beside the Afon Biga.

Common Land

Most medieval villages had several acres on the edge of the settlement set aside for the use of the villagers, but all this common land was actually privately owned, either by the Lord of the Manor, collectively by the local villagers or, perhaps, even by a city corporation. What is held 'in common' by certain local individuals or their families is the right to use this land. If you were such a tenant, you were known as a 'commoner', and, as such,

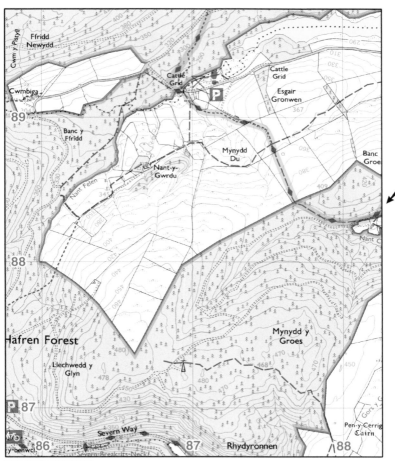

Contours are given in metres
The vertical interval is 10m

had rights: 'of pasture' – to graze specified livestock; 'of estovers' – to gather and take wood (but not fell trees); 'in the soil' – to take sand, coal or minerals; 'of turbary' – to dig peat for fuel; and 'of piscary' – to catch fish from ponds or streams. These rights extended only to that which the ground produced naturally, i.e. there was no right to plant crops, and there were often seasonal limitations. Usually 'Bye Law men' were appointed annually from among the tenants of the common, and it was their job to care for hedges, gates, drains and ditches. Expenses incurred in this task were presented to the annual meeting each year, and each tenant contributed an equal proportion in payment.

8 Afon Biga to Aberhosan
Afon Biga i Aberhosan

9 ¹/₂ miles (14.75 km)

Cross the Afon Biga and continue along the road, passing a cattle grid and then turning right **A** along a forest track for about a mile (1.6 km). Bear a little to the left and walk, initially with the trees to your left, following the waymark posts. Soon the track rises and enters trees, then a little footbridge takes you over a stream, and you continue, walking up a green track through a forestry plantation, where the undergrowth is sumptuous and mossy, interspersed with bilberry bushes. At the top of the track you join a road and turn right, soon passing through an area of felled trees. The pleasant view reveals some tempting higher peaks beyond.

You then pass a cattle grid and leave Hafren Forest on a route shared with National Cycle Route **8**, passing a weather station and continuing along the road and crossing the bridge over the Afon Lwyd. Follow the road as it swings right and climbs and, at the top of the hill and just before the road swings gently away to the right, turn off left along a track. Go through a gate and continue along a farm track to reach a gate. Go through this and veer off slightly to the left of the track which leads to the farmhouse, walking over rough ground to reach a footbridge. Cross this and walk up to a stile, which you climb and carry on ahead. Join a track and bear left to follow it as it then swings around to the right to reach a gate (ignore the track which branches off to the left). Go through the gate and continue along the track, passing a small quarry to your left. The landscape is now becoming one of open moorland, broken with dense forest plantations. A fence joins from the right and you walk towards the corner post of the fence to turn half-right when you reach it, proceeding down to a gateway below. Go through the gate and turn left, to walk with the hedge on your left.

Cross two stiles and a bridge and continue ahead, with the fence now away to your left. The gate you are now heading towards can be reached by following the line of electricity poles. Go through the gate, cross a track and continue ahead. Pass through two more gates in front of Llwyn y Gog Farm **B** and walk along the pleasant green track overlooking a broad and similarly green valley. When you reach two gates, go through them

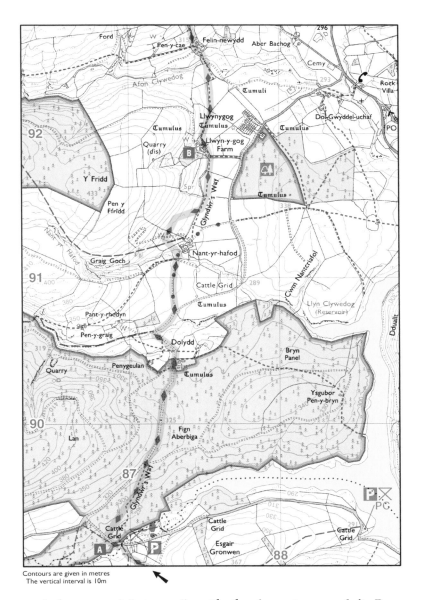

Contours are given in metres
The vertical interval is 10m

and then veer left to walk with the fence to your left. Pass through another gate and continue ahead towards a stile. Cross this and walk down a fairly steep bank to a lane. Go through a gate, cross a bridge, go through a second gate and continue. When the road bends right towards Felin-newydd, continue

Descending westwards from Foel Fadian along Glyndŵr's Way, having just passed Glaslyn. If you have time, you can walk around the lake in about one hour.

ahead, climbing a steep grassy slope to a stile. Cross this stile and a second one on the other side of the track, and then continue around a green mound to walk up a hollow lane. Continue climbing up this lovely green hollow way to reach a waymark post, where you turn left to cross a stile, and then turn right. Walk up to a second stile, climb it and continue ahead across the field to a waymark post. When you reach the post continue ahead to a stile. Cross this and veer to the left to walk with a fence on your right.

As you approach Dylife you cross a high undulating plateau with excellent views of the surrounding mountains, although your immediate surroundings are just tussocky grass conspicuously inhabited by sheep, but enlivened with birdsong including an almost unbroken chorus of skylarks during the spring. Climb a stile beside the next gate and carry on, now with the fence on your left. The track you are walking along is quite ancient; the exposed rock has been worn down by the passage of innumerable cart wheels. You round a corner and the few remaining houses of Dylife **23** come into view when you pass a post at a track junction. Turn right here if you wish to leave Glyndŵr's Way to descend the hill and, perhaps, visit The Star Inn, where you can enjoy real ale and a decent meal in very amenable surroundings.

It seems certain that mining took place at Dylife during Roman times, with a substantial revival occurring at the start of the 18th century. The Company of Mine Adventurers reported shafts at 'Delivia' in 1691, although the mine suffered from flooding, but it was not until 150 years later, with the discovery of the Llechwedd Ddu lode, that the mine enjoyed its most productive period. In 1851, 300 men, women and children were employed here, when the largest waterwheel ever erected in Wales, known as the Martha, was used for pumping and drawing. Its diameter was 63 feet (19.2 metres). When the mine was taken over by a new company it was equipped with the most up-to-date machinery in the country, including colliery-style winding cages. The Boundary Shaft was pumped using a 60-inch (152-cm) Cornish steam engine, with drawing being achieved using a 50-foot (15-metre) waterwheel situated over a mile away. How the problems of friction, weather and signalling were overcome on this installation still remains a mystery. The mine's best year was 1863, when 2,571 tons of lead ore were raised, a record second only to Van mine (see the previous chapter). The village of Dylife at this

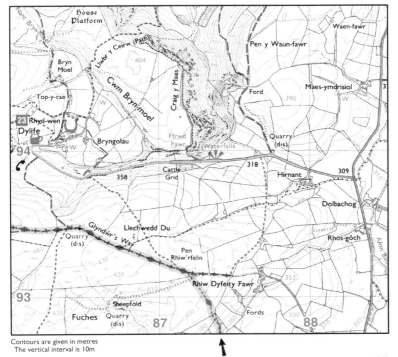

Contours are given in metres
The vertical interval is 10m

time had a post office, a school, several pubs and, of course, several chapels. Within ten years, however, the mine's output rapidly declined and its owners, wisely trading on past success, managed to sell it for £73,000, a vast sum at the time. The decline continued in spite of new works, and the Dylife enterprise finally ceased operations in 1884.

Continuing on the track, or rejoining it if you have made the diversion to Dylife, you pass through a ffridd (enclosure) to cross a stile beside a gate, and carry straight on. You are following a green track which crosses high, undulating moorland, with views of Dylife down to the right, a fine valley ahead and to the right, while behind is the vast wind farm on Trannon Moor, above Carno. You continue climbing towards the Roman fortlet **24**, on a track which is almost certainly very ancient, with the undulating summits of the Pumlumon range to the left. You pass a stile beside a gateway and continue along a green track. Soon you pass an elaborate TV aerial to the right, while to your left are the low embankments which were once topped by the walls of the fortlet at Penycrocbren, a remote outpost of the Roman Empire. Penycrocbren translates as 'gallows hill', and was the scene of a grisly discovery in the 1930s, when a skull in a cage was unearthed. It was the head of the mine blacksmith, who over two centuries before had killed his wife and daughter and thrown their bodies down a mineshaft. His crime was discovered and he was tried, found guilty and then forced to make his own gibbet

Looking down the Dulas Valley towards Machynlleth.

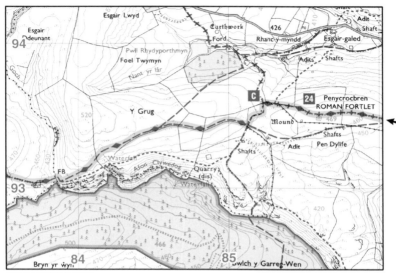

Contours are given in metres
The vertical interval is 10m

cages, before being executed. The corpse was then left on display, as a warning to others. The skull and the gibbet are now displayed in the Welsh Folk Museum at St Fagan's, Cardiff.

Continue ahead, now descending very gently with some of the mining remains of Dylife visible to the right. Cross a stile beside a gate and continue ahead towards a waymark post. When you reach this post **C**, which is by a gate and a stile, do not cross them but veer left as directed by the waymark post and follow a track as it bears around to the right leading you to a gate. Go through this and continue ahead along a track for a short distance and, just before reaching two isolated gateposts, turn right through a small gate and continue up the hill with a small bank to your left. Continue with the bank alongside as it bends a little to the left before bearing right and leading up to a bridle gate. When you reach the gate, go through it and bear just slightly left to continue with the bank still to your left. To the right are the shallow slopes of Y Grug, while on the left there are areas of new forest plantation, with the hill-tops beyond. In the cwm to the left is the infant Afon Clywedog, which feeds the reservoir passed earlier on Glyndŵr's Way.

Eventually the bank on the left, which has accompanied the route for the last mile or so, turns down into the cwm, but you continue ahead along the clear path. Go through a gate and

The remote Glaslyn, with Foel Fadian in the background.

continue to follow the path. Another minor path eventually joins from the left by a waymark post and you can, if you wish, make a short diversion along this to catch a glimpse of the waterfalls, and then return to this point. Continue ahead and start a steep zig-zag descent (be careful in wet weather, it can be slippery) to a bridge, which you cross before going through a gate. Continue uphill along the path with waterfalls and a wood to your left. Again, take care if the ground is wet (although wet weather does make the falls more spectacular). At the top of the short climb veer to the right to reach a way-mark post by a fence corner. Now walk as directed, with the fence to your left. Cross a stile and follow the track, until another waymark post appears. When you reach the post, fork left and you soon pass the spoil heaps and faint remains of the Cyfarthfa mine **25**. This was an unsuccessful venture which began around 1842 and ended – having produced only 100 tons of lead and copper ore – with a lawsuit in the Court of Chancery around 1878, when the diversion of water for the use of the mine was considered to be to the detriment of fulling mills near Machynlleth. As you continue along the track you can see, over to the left, the broken dam of the lake, itself fed by a long leat and a 'cut and cover' tunnel from Glaslyn, which once fed water to the mine machinery.

Continue to walk on to reach a waymark post, where you rejoin the track and turn left. As you follow the track look out for a waymark post which directs you to leave the main track and bear to the right along a green track which leads to another waymark post, where you again veer right following a fainter green track. The distinct path disappears, but you maintain your direction over the heather, couch grass and bilberries to eventually reach a fence, where you turn right.

You now follow a track beside a fence, with Glaslyn away to the left. The mountain directly ahead of you is Foel Fadian **26**, 1,850 feet (564 metres) high. There is a fine route around Glaslyn **27** and, in spite of its appearance, this diversion through the nature reserve would take you less than an hour. Pass a cattle grid by the entrance to the reserve and continue ahead and, as the track swings gently to the right, the view down the cwm of Nant Fadian begins to open up. Although there are no remains to be seen, you are close to what must have been one of the most remote and inaccessible mines in the district, worked in the 1870s by Captain Edward Williams of Dylife. It is reported that the Moel Fadian mine produced just 25 tons of copper ore. Now look out for the waymark post on your left **D**, which directs you to turn left along a track which is, in places, wet. You

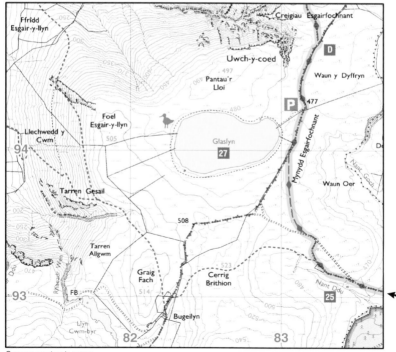

Contours are given in metres
The vertical interval is 10m

follow the track over a low summit as it bends to the left, where you reach the highest point on Glyndŵr's Way, and descends beside the cwm. A spectacular view confronts you and, on a very clear day, you can see Cardigan Bay.

The path initially descends very steeply and the track, which is cut into the bedrock, can become very slippery in wet weather. Do take care here – often you can avoid slippery sections by walking to one side. The view ahead now is quite stunning. When you reach a waymark post, stay on the main track, which turns to the left and continues downhill. You cross the course of a stream (which can run quite strongly after wet weather) and continue along the track for a mile (1.6 km), still descending downhill and zig-zagging to a gate. Go through the gate and carry on along what is now a green track. Pass through another gate and continue along a superb example of a

The aerogenerator above the Centre for Alternative Technology, from Glaslyn Gorge. You have just passed the remains of the remote Moel Fadian mine.

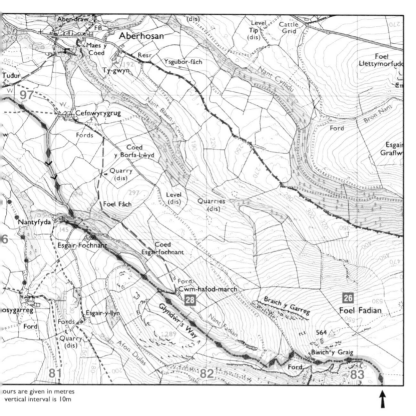

ours are given in metres
vertical interval is 10m

green track above a steep valley lined with woodland, and still with a wonderful view of mountains ahead. Down in the valley, almost hidden from view, is the pretty cottage of Cwm-hafod-march **28**, a single-storey building originally used as a shepherd's summer residence. Go through a gate and continue ahead – after the wildness around Dylife, it is extremely pleasant to walk along this charming, verdant valley.

You pass a small caravan park to the left to go through a gate and walk by the house of Esgair-Fochnant. Continue along the track, which descends and makes a hairpin turn by Nantyfyda. Continue along the road, ignoring a gate to the left, and following it as it swings left uphill, passing a waymark post. When the road forks, go to the right, walking steeply uphill. Red kites can often be seen here, wheeling around effortlessly on thermals as they lazily stalk their prey. The tiny village of Aberhosan lies a short distance ahead along the road, beyond Cefnwyrygrug Farm.

The Drovers' Roads

Above Dylife, Glyndŵr's Way, as it does in many other places, follows parts of an old drovers' route. Well before the cowboys herded their cattle over the dusty plains of America, the Welsh drove their black cattle, sheep, pigs, geese and latterly turkeys (these last two with their feet encased in 'boots' of tar) hundreds of miles to the rich markets of southern England. These noisy cavalcades were driven across the hills at a steady two miles per hour from the time of the Norman Conquest right up until the late 19th century. The scene was described thus in 1926:

> A great feature of the droves was the noise they made. It was heard for miles and warned local farmers what to expect. The noise consisted of the shouting of the drovers combined with a certain amount of noise from the cattle. But it was the men's voices that chiefly attracted attention. It was something out of the common, neither shouting, calling, crying, singing, halloing or anything else, but a noise of itself, apparently made to carry and capable of arresting the countryside. The horsemen and two of the cattle acted as leaders to the rest, and the men kept calling and shouting the whole time. As soon as the local farmers heard the noise they rushed their cattle out of the way, for if once they got into the drove, they could not easily be got out again.

The great droves of cattle and sheep could be strung out over half a mile, and their journey, for example from North Wales to Kent, could take three weeks. The drovers, on horseback, were ably assisted by their dogs – corgis – whose low build enabled them to snap at the beasts to encourage their progress and avoid the ensuing kick! When the drove was over the dogs would often then make their own way home ahead of the men. Indeed, the women would prepare for the men's return a couple of days after the dogs appeared.

Drovers, for the most part, had a reputation for honesty, since the stock they moved was not paid for until it was sold at market – they would then return to Wales with the money, which was distributed to the farmers, less commission.

During the reigns of Edward VI and Elizabeth I statutes were passed which required the drovers to be licensed. To obtain such a licence a man had to be married, a householder and over 30 years old. During the reign of Queen Anne a statute was enacted which made it impossible for a drover to declare himself bankrupt, thus obliging him to keep to any contracts undertaken. In addition, stock could not be moved on the Sabbath, and drovers often fell foul of this rule. It was not unusual for their journeys to recommence at one minute past midnight on a Monday, with the cattle and sheep being rounded up ready for a dawn start.

Moving over what were, for the times, vast distances, the drovers carried with them the latest news. The story of the British victory at Waterloo in 1815 was spread to the Welsh hills by drovers, along with tales of a better life in the New World, of new mechanical inventions, and even cuttings of fruits unheard of in Wales. By the end of the 18th century the drovers had created an effective banking system, in order to avoid the risk of robbery in what was still a countryside without effective policing.

It was the building of the railways which finally ended this centuries-old practice, but it is worth looking out for the clues which reveal these ancient routes as you progress along Glyndŵr's Way: lanes or tracks with walls or hedges set widely apart, or unusually wide verges where the stock once grazed.

Looking east from the Roman fortlet of Penycrocbren, above Dylife. The mountain tracks hereabouts must be very ancient.

9 Aberhosan to Machynlleth
Aberhosan i Fachynlleth

9 ¹/₂ miles (15.25 km)

When the road south-west of Cefnwyrygrug swings to the right, you turn off left **A** through a gate and follow the track. Pass through another gate and continue ahead, following the track as it bends left and then swings right, passing a waymark post. Go through a gate to enter a rougher tree-lined section and continue downhill to a road, where you turn right. You are now walking along one side of a steep valley, with trees all around and the pleasant gurgling sounds of a stream, which feeds the Afon Hengwm, below and to the left. When you join a road which approaches from the left, continue ahead, passing a telephone box. About 50 yards further on, at the next road junction, turn left to cross a bridge and pass through a gateway, then continue ahead up the hill.

The road, continuing to climb, bends at first to the left and then to the right. Go through the gate at Cleriau-isaf **B** and immediately turn right. Pass through a second gate between barns and then turn left to leave the farmyard through a gate. Continue along the track, enjoying a very fine view to your right. Climb to a gate, go through and veer right along the track. Pass

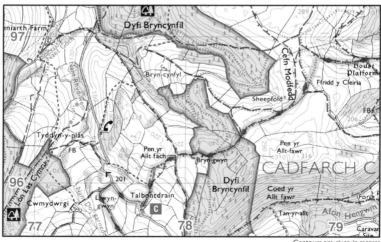

Contours are given in metres
The vertical interval is 10m

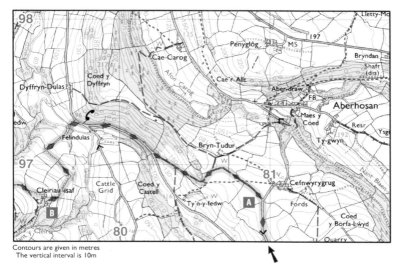

Contours are given in metres
The vertical interval is 10m

through a gate and continue, still gently climbing, and then go through another gate and continue along the track, still with an excellent view to your right. Yet another gate appears: go through and continue climbing along the main track as it bends around to the left. When the track splits, go through the gateway ahead, by a small plantation of trees. You are now sharing the bridleway with a Machynlleth Mountain Biking route, so watch out for riders.

Go through a gateway and, with the main track swinging around to the right, continue straight ahead along a green track, with a fence to your left and passing a waymark post. Again you are gently climbing. Continue over the summit and carry on along the green track, still with the fence to your left. Pass through a gate and follow the track into a forest plantation. When you reach a forest road, cross it and continue on down to a gate and stile ahead, and go through. Bear right along the track, then take the right fork as waymarked. You pass a tidy stone barn to the left and carry on through a small gate ahead. Follow the track downhill to a waymark post and walk across a field in the general direction of the furthest white house on the hillside ahead. The track soon becomes clearer and swings to the left towards Talbontdrain. Pass through a gate and walk down the track. Ford a small stream and continue up the track. Go through a gate and pass the guest house at Talbontdrain (B&B) to walk up to the road **C**, where you turn right.

Looking over Talbontdrain from Rhiw Goch. Although Machynlleth is not far away, the area still feels very remote.

The road now climbs, swinging first to the left and then to the right. Turn off left, as waymarked, at the entrance to Llwyn-gwyn to follow the main Glyndŵr's Way path, which is signed to the left (there is a short alternative route here, signed to the right). Go through a gate and continue with a fence to your left to the next gate, which you go through and carry on ahead to yet another gate, which you also go through, and carry on climbing. When the main track swings around to the left (it is chained off here), you carry on ahead as waymarked to reach a gate. Go through this and walk ahead, climbing quite steeply now up a track, following the waymark posts. You climb very steeply up to a fenced area of forest, and turn left at the top to walk with the fence on your right. The views are stunning: a panorama of hills stretching north. At the top of the track climb the stile beside a gate and turn right. You have now once again joined one of the Machynlleth Mountain Biking routes, this time at a notorious stretch known as 'The Chute' **29**: a very steep and testing downhill section over loose rock and wet and slippery slate – so, again, watch out: cyclists may approach you very quickly from behind here!

As you emerge from the trees a track forks off to the right, but you continue ahead with the fence to your right. Go through a gate and continue with the fence to your right, and a fine view over the valley to your left. The track maintains its height as it traverses the hillside. You go through a gate and continue with a fence to your left. When the fence ends, continue ahead along the track, which gets very wet before the next gate. However, you can find a way around, and go through the gate and continue. Pass through another couple of gates and continue along the track. Trees appear on your left as you reach a T-junction **D**, where you turn right and take the gate to the left, to follow the green path (ignoring the gate to the right).

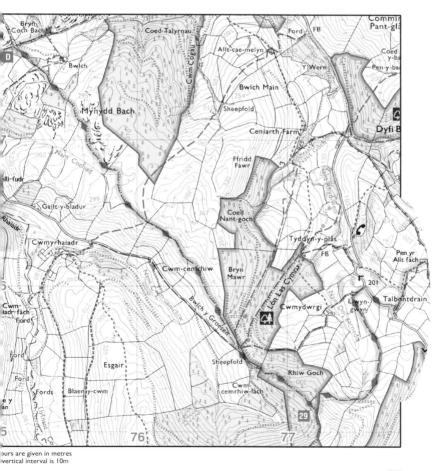

ours are given in metres
vertical interval is 10m

Continue on a faint green path as it zig-zags steeply downhill. Look out for a waymark post, where you turn sharp left to climb uphill along a track which then swings around to the right over a large patch of exposed rock and continues uphill. Ignore a path that breaks away to the left and carry on uphill. You reach a stile and cross it to enter a forestry plantation. Now follow the clear track ahead, surrounded and overshadowed by tall, mature conifers.

You pass several waymark posts on your left as you walk ahead along the track, until it becomes rougher and narrower.

The peaks of Tarren y Gesail and Cadair Idris, beyond the Afon Dyfi, from Cefn Modfedd. You are likely to see mountain-bikers around here.

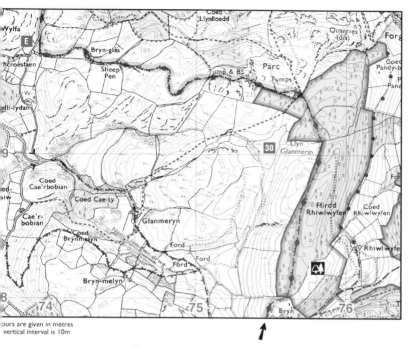

You come to another waymark post where you join another track, still continuing straight ahead. When the track dog-legs, look out for a waymark post which directs you to continue directly ahead through a gap in a stone wall. The track has now become a narrow path that twists and turns, now with tall trees to the right, and younger forestry to the left. Leave the plantation through a gate and follow the waymarked path ahead, with superb views over the Dyfi Valley, a lone aero-generator prominent on a hilltop ahead, and Llyn Glanmerin **30** below you to the left. You now follow a clear path uphill and through bracken. Ignore a path to your left and carry on ahead, veering right to a gate. Go through and follow the clear track downhill, with Machynlleth now in full view ahead, spread over the valley floor. Pass a waymark post and continue. When you reach two gates ahead, go through the left-hand one and continue along the track. After about 50 yards you join another rough track, and continue ahead. Pass Bryn-glas and, about 100 yards beyond, veer left to a gate. Go through and continue. The track descends through woods, swings around to the right and goes through a gate to join a road **E**, where you continue ahead.

The Parliament House and Tourist Information Centre in Machynlleth, opposite the entrance to The Plas, where Glyndŵr's Way emerges onto Heol Maengwyn.

As the road descends and veers to the left, follow the track straight ahead. Ignore a gate to your right and continue on towards Machynlleth. Cross the track below Cae-Gybi Cottages and carry on downhill. You pass through a kissing-gate and continue along a defined path, which is quite steep and can be slippery. Carefully descend the Roman Steps **31**, carved from the living slate (but perhaps not by the Romans) and very slippery when wet, to reach another kissing-gate. Go through and walk ahead towards the road. Just before you reach the road, turn right through gates to enter the grounds of Y Plas (or you can leave the official route to join the road and turn right to walk to the clock-tower, and then turn right again to see most of the shops in the town). Now follow the track as waymarked, eventually crossing in front of Y Plas **32** and passing the commemorative Glyndŵr's stone. Y Plas was, until 1948, the country seat of the Marquis of Londonderry, but is now the home of 'Celtica', a visitor centre presenting the history and culture of the Celts. At the heart of the exhibition is a mystical audio-visual journey, where Nia and her brother Gwydion take you on a journey to discover the re-awakening of the Celtic spirit. Bear right in front of the Bro Ddyfi Leisure Centre and follow the path as waymarked, eventually passing through wrought-iron gates to reach the Owain Glyndŵr Centre, by the Tourist Information Centre, in Maengwyn Street.

The handsome market town of Machynlleth marks the lowest crossing on the Afon Dyfi, so it is in a way almost a coastal town – spring tides claw their way up the river as far as Pennal, a Roman settlement a couple of miles below the Dyfi Bridge. It is geograph-ically pretty much at the centre of Wales and, with due respect to Cardiff, as fair a place as you could imagine for its capital.

This point was not wasted on Owain Glyndŵr, who did indeed make the town his capital in 1404, when he had himself crowned King of a free Wales at the Parliament House in Maengwyn Street (it has been rebuilt since then). A memorial, which you passed outside Plas Machynlleth, was ceremonially

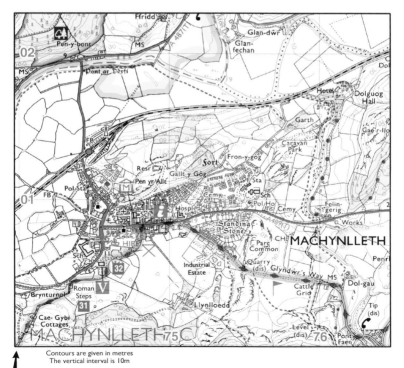

Contours are given in metres
The vertical interval is 10m

uncovered on 16 September 2000, marking 600 years since the start of his short-lived and ultimately unsuccessful revolt against the English Crown. Royal House, a stone's throw from the clock-tower, is said to be where Owain Glyndŵr resided when he held his parliament in Machynlleth. Dafydd Gam was imprisoned in a cellar here after he attempted to assassinate Owain. It took the name Royal House after Charles I stayed there in 1644 on a journey to Chester. An informal local 'parliament' was held from the 1920s to the 1940s in William Lewis' saddler's shop behind the town clock. The elders of the town debated local, national and international affairs, sitting on benches and boxes in a semi-circle in order of seniority. Meanwhile the saddler continued to stitch his leatherwork.

Try to find time to visit The Tabernacl Museum of Modern Art, Wales, which has six fine exhibition spaces, with free admission. The adjacent auditorium has excellent acoustics and seating for 400 people, and there are regular performances by visiting musicians, as well as a truly splendid festival in late August, when many well-known performers are featured. Events range from recitals for children to jazz, and a lively Fringe provides further variety. Purchased by Andrew Lambert in 1984, The Tabernacl opened as simply a beautiful auditorium in 1986. Much work followed and eventually buildings next door were taken over and converted into an art gallery. Its expansion continues, with the old tannery soon to be incorporated.

Having seen the sights of Machynlleth you might feel you need some refreshment. The town has a wide choice of pubs, inns and cafés, the most imposing of these being The Wynnstay in Maengwyn Street. It is a comfortable, friendly and welcoming hotel, once visited by Lloyd George amongst others, with excellent accommodation, hospitable bars with a choice of real ales, and an outstanding chef. Next door is Greenstiles, where you can obtain any outdoor gear, boots or cagoules you might need. Further down Maengwyn Street you'll find the Tourist Information Centre, and they can give you details of accommodation in the area, along with all the other things you would expect. Recently Machynlleth was lauded as one of the top 32 places in Britain 'not to be missed'. It is truly remarkable that this little town, right in the heart of rural Wales, has become a vibrant and stylish centre not only of local life, but of art, culture and walking. Machynlleth is an excellent place to break your journey for a day or two, to rest, recuperate and enjoy the attractions.

Enjoying the summer sunshine in Machynlleth. At times like these this little town seems very cosmopolitan.

Fascinating and life-changing displays at the Centre for Alternative Technology. The café and bookshop are also both excellent, so try to make the time to visit.

The Centre for Alternative Technology

This is one of Wales' leading visitor attractions, and an immeasurable asset to Machynlleth. Unfortunately you can't really make the short journey north to Pantperthog by footpath, where 'the Quarry', as it is known, is situated, but you can still enjoy a walk, mainly along quiet roads, crossing the striking new Millennium Cycle Bridge on the way. Head north from the town, passing the station, then follow the new riverside cycleway which leaves the road to the right by the Dyfi Bridge. Soon you'll cross the river and emerge onto a main road. Follow this for a short distance, then turn right at Fridd Gate, by the old toll house (signed to Llanwrin). Cross the bridge over the Afon Dulas (pronounced 'dilas') and turn left along the single-track road. This will bring you to the CAT. You can ride up to the exhibition and gardens on a water-powered cliff railway, which was built in 1992 and modelled upon the Victorian construction at Linton in Devon. It stands on the site of the original quarry railway.

The old Llwyngwern slate quarry was worked here until 1951, a year after the owner was killed by a falling stone. Until then large families lived on the site, and it is recorded there were 'no amenities whatsoever . . . people lived poor, pathetic lives.' Once abandoned, it became a lost, romantic place, remembered only by a few locals. In 1973 Gerard Morgan-Grenville, CAT's founder and a successful businessman, had become disenchanted with the way society was behaving towards its surroundings and resources, and decided to do something about it. The old quarry, now rapidly becoming ever more wildly overgrown, seemed to be the ideal site upon which to realise this dream. Fortunately the then owners, John and Audrey Beaumont, were both sympathetic to his vision. And so it all began.

Today, the ideas that the CAT promotes are entering the mainstream, and our lives are gradually (some would say too gradually) becoming shaped by ideas of energy conservation and recycling. These days the exhibition is wonderful, inspirational: but in any project with such high ideals things do not shape up easily, and in the early days it was decidedly shaky. The Quarry's fortunes have ebbed and flowed over the years, but it has always been driven by an ideal that was fundamentally sound. Today it makes a splendid day out: there is an excellent vegetarian/wholefood restaurant, a book and gift shop, and it is to be hoped that you will leave full of life-changing ideas.

10 Machynlleth to Cemmaes Road
Machynlleth i Lantwymyn

8 ³/₄ miles (14.25 km)

From the Owain Glyndŵr Centre in Machynlleth walk along
Maengwyn Street in the direction of Newtown. When you reach
the Bro Dyfi Community Hospital **A** on the left, turn right as
signed towards Dylife and walk along Treowain, passing the
Health Centre and the Treowain Enterprise Park. Continue
ahead along the road as you pass the last house on the left and
begin gently climbing. Pass a cattle grid and follow the road as
it traverses the golf course. On your left is a small obelisk in an
enclosure: it is part of the Ordnance Survey's Global Positioning
System. You leave the golf course over a second cattle grid and
follow the road as it swings to the right by a waymark post.

Stay on the main road as you enter the village of Forge **33**,
turning left and then right over the bridge (do not go straight
ahead), passing a telephone kiosk and staying on the road,
which you are sharing with National Cycle Route **8**. Forge once
supported five fulling mills, or pandys, the last of which closed
in 1937, and there was at one time a small electricity generating
station by Dolgau Farm, set up in 1931. The village has been
famous amongst bee-keepers for many years, thanks to the
efforts of Alfred Evans, who regularly broadcast on the subject.

Pass the house Dolhan on the right and turn left **B** along a
lane. When the lane dips slightly and passes under electricity
cables before bending to the left, you turn right to follow a
track. Go through a gate and continue ahead, climbing gently
and swinging first to the right and then to the left. Just before
the gate at Pen-rhos-bâch climb up the bank on your right to
cross a stile. Head for the obvious telegraph pole, descend the
bank and continue to reach a stile beside a gate. Cross this and
carry on ahead towards a waymark post. Veer slightly left at
the post, pass under electricity cables and continue on to
another post a short distance ahead. Continue, as directed,
across a field and head down towards the left-hand corner,
where you cross a muddy patch between trees to reach a gate
ahead. Turn left and go through. Pass through a second gate
and turn right along a farm road. Go through a gate, walk
down to a road and turn left.

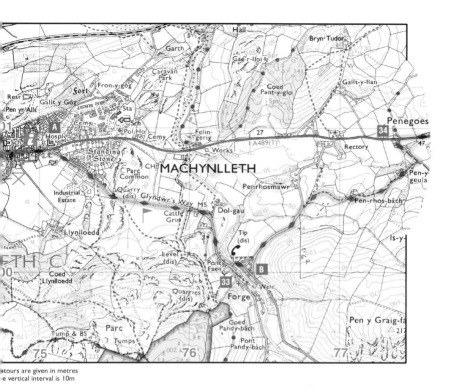

tours are given in metres
e vertical interval is 10m

Walk along the road, crossing a bridge and passing the beautifully restored and working 17th-century water mill, where the adjoining buildings are now used for holiday accommodation. When you reach the main road, turn right. The village of Penegoes **34**, harassed by the main road, has ancient connections with the Princes of Powys; nearby Dolguog is associated with the fortress, long since disappeared, of Owain Cyfeiliog, the ruler and poet who died in 1197. Just over the hedge, and right by the main road, is an ancient healing well. If you walk back a short distance along the road towards Machynlleth you will find the church, beyond which is a grove of oaks where the head of Egeos, the Celtic saint who gave his name to the village (Penegoes = head of Egeos) is said to be buried. The rectory was the birthplace of Richard Wilson (1714–82), a landscape artist, and was later visited by Felicia Dorothea Hemans (1793–1835) who wrote the much-abused poem 'Casabianca', containing the line: 'The boy stood on the burning deck'. She came here to visit her brother-in-law, who was rector.

Looking north over the Dyfi Valley towards Cadair Idris from Bryn-wg Common.

Leave Penegoes along the road, ignoring the first turning to the right and then, 50 yards further on, forking right along a lane by houses and continuing out of the village. Fork right by Maesperthi, as directed by the waymark post, to walk up a rougher track towards Maesllwyni. When a farm track joins from the right, continue ahead to reach a gate. Go through and carry on along the track to go through another gate and continue gently uphill for about half a mile (0.8 km). You are now progressing up a cwm, with a stream down to your right and a fine view over Penegoes behind you, against a backdrop of the rolling hills of the Dyfi Valley. Still climbing, you pass a small stand of conifers on the right and reach a gate: go through and continue ahead. Eventually you reach two more gates. Take the left-hand one and turn sharp left to climb steeply uphill, with a fence to your left. Initially the climb is quite hard work, but the summit is soon reached and then you are gently descending, with a very fine view over the Dyfi Valley: the tiny village directly ahead and across the river is Llanwrin, where the Early English style St Gwrin's Church has a handsome rood screen and some stained glass dating from 1461. The original church was dedicated to the saints Ust and Dyfrig, who came here from Brittany in AD 516. Canon Silvan Evans, who lived in the rectory from 1876 to 1903, compiled the Welsh dictionary and was the first Welsh lecturer at Aberystwyth University.

You reach a very large ladder-stile, beneath which two fences cross. Climb this and now walk, with the fence to your right, through rough pasture, looking out for the waymark post ahead. When you reach it, continue, still with the fence to your right and a magnificent view over the valley, towards the next post. Carry on ahead, leaving the bracken and gorse behind for a while, before entering another patch of it.

Eventually a waymark post appears amidst more bracken, and you are directed to bear right. When the fence veers slightly further to the right, continue as directed by the waymark post, dipping steeply down to find a stile, which can be hidden by the bracken during the summer. Cross this and climb up to another waymark post. Walk ahead, with the fence still to your right. As you cross a farm track look for a waymark post which directs you to cross a stile and bear left along a rough path through more bracken, above a little cwm to the right. Very soon you reach a waymark post **C**, where you turn right at a path junction.

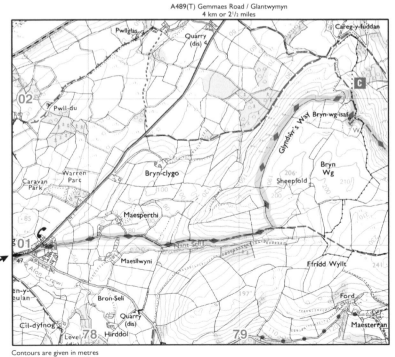

A489(T) Gemmaes Road / Glantwymyn
4 km or 2¹/₂ miles

Contours are given in metres
The vertical interval is 10m

Below you and ahead is the village of Abercegir, nestling at a junction of three steep valleys. Cross a tiny stream and continue ahead, enjoying stunning views all around. The narrow path you are following dips into a cwm, crosses a stream emerging from trees and climbs to a waymark post. Carry on, with a fence to your right as you gradually descend the hillside. Cross another small stream and continue ahead (do not go uphill). Below you, to the left, is Factory Isaf. Follow the path as it zig-zags downhill to a small gate, which you go through to walk along a shady and hedged green lane. When this joins a farm track by a cattle grid and a waymark post, continue ahead. Turn left off the track as waymarked, to walk to the left of Yr Hen Felin (B&B and excellent food), cross a bridge and follow the path to the right, which gives you a fine view of the remains of the waterwheel, before you reach the road. Turn left and walk along the road for about 50 yards to a junction, where you turn sharp right by Top y Pentre and walk along the road, gently climbing to leave Abercegir.

Now look out for a track which joins from the left and turn sharp left here, following this as it climbs gently uphill and swings to the right. When you approach the top of the track, turn left through a small gate, then turn right and walk with the fence to your right. Ignore the first gate on your right and walk up to the second gate in the top right-hand field corner, and go through. Now walk uphill with a wall to your left, passing through a gate and enjoying the fine view which opens up to your left beyond the wall. Ignore a field gate to your left and continue ahead through a gap in the hedge. Go through a bridle gate and carry on, still climbing with the fence and hedge to your left. Go through another bridle gate and veer slightly right around the hill, still climbing. The view is now more expansive, with Llanwrin nestling in the Dyfi Valley and a single aerogenerator on the hill behind it.

When you come to a bridle gate in a stone wall, go through and walk half-right uphill, gradually leaving the wall away to your left as you again swing around the hill. Soon you join a farm road coming in from the right, and you now follow this, still climbing with the summit of Rhôs y Silio up to your right. The track passes through a gateway as you carry on ahead, still climbing. To the north the summit of Cadair Idris has now become visible, and to the north-east the competing summit of Aran Fawddwy is also prominent.

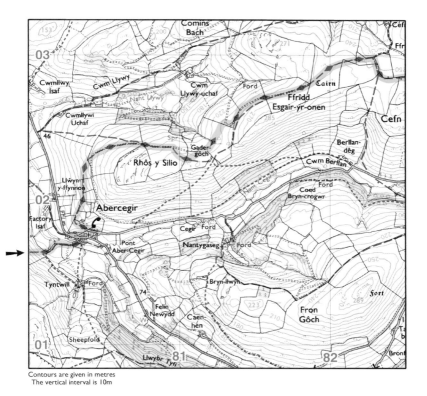

Contours are given in metres
The vertical interval is 10m

The track eventually swings slightly right and peters out in a field; you continue ahead to a gate: go through and then bear slightly left towards trees. Look out for the waymark post, which stands amongst the remnants of an old hedge-line and, when you reach this, veer left as directed towards the next post, and then carry on, now with the summit of Aran Fawddwy on the horizon directly ahead. Go through a gate and turn right to follow a green track around the edge of the field, with the fence to your right. Pass through another gate and walk ahead along a broad green track, with a fence to your left. As you progress, look back for a view of the Afon Dyfi, a salmon and sea trout river, glistening in the sun. The track is delightful, carpeted with deep grass and carved into the high slope of Cefn Coch. Ahead is the Cemmaes Ridge, topped by a spread of large aerogenerators which comprise the Cemmaes Wind Farm. The hills are speckled with sheep and patterned with the remains of stone walls, and all is utter peace.

When you reach a gate, go through and continue, veering just slightly left across an open field and enjoying an opening view along the broad valley towards Dinas Mawddwy. The field is quite wet and marshy in places. Eventually a waymark post appears just beyond a fence corner, and you walk towards it. Carry on ahead as directed by the next post towards a stone wall which joins your route from the left. Walk beside this towards a waymark post by a track. Cross a tiny stream, join the track and turn right to walk uphill. Go through a gate and continue straight ahead towards another gate, which you also go through and then bear left, to walk with a low wall and a fence to your left. When you reach a wooden gate, go through and carry on with the wall still to your left, to reach yet another gate, which you go through, to walk beside a now intact wall. When you reach two gates in the field corner, go through the left-hand one to walk down a green track. Pass a gate to your left and continue ahead. Pass through a gate to emerge at the top of a lane where you turn left **D**.

About a mile south of this point, along the track to your right, is the ancient settlement of Darowen **35**, and tucked away in the Ffernant Valley, half a mile south-east of this village, is old Pwlliwrch, the hidden farm where some think Owain Glyndŵr ended his days. In the field ahead of you at the track junction is Maen Llwyd, one of two survivors of the three stones which once marked out an area of sanctuary around Darowen, and which aligns, through the churchyard and the other surviving stone, with one of the five summits of Pumlumon.

Walk downhill and, when the lane veers left, carry on ahead, crossing a waymarked stile on your right. Maintain your direction across the field to reach a stile in the fence ahead. Cross the stile and carry on to the next, which you again cross, then continue over the brow of the hill, keeping the steep valley to your left, to reach another stile. Cross this and carry on ahead down towards Cemmaes Road. As you approach a fence, and just before a small enclosure, look to your right to pick out a stile. Cross this and then turn left to descend along a track, passing a last resting place for veteran tractors, gracefully and picturesquely decaying. Go through a gate and descend to the main road. Cross a stile beside a gate and turn left to walk beside the road to Cemmaes Road, where there is a village shop and post office, and a very quiet pub.

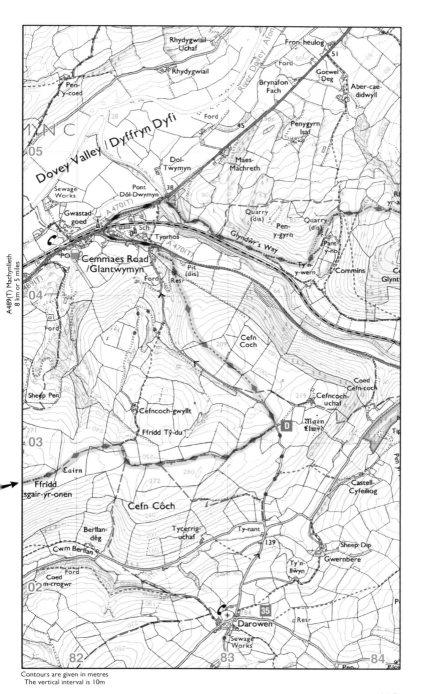

Contours are given in metres
The vertical interval is 10m

113

11 Cemmaes Road to Llanbrynmair
Glantwymyn i Lanbrynmair

6 ³/₄ miles (10.75 km)

From the roundabout in Cemmaes Road walk along the road towards Dolgellau, crossing first the railway and then the Afon Twymyn, before turning immediately sharp right **A** through a gate and continuing along a drive, passing a very fine brick railway arch over the river, to your right. Continue climbing gently uphill, with tall trees on your left. Go through the next gate and carry on, with low scattered stands of trees on your left and the railway and the steep river valley to your right; the main road is, thankfully, well hidden amongst trees. When you reach a fork in the track, at a waymark post, go left and continue gently uphill. The track swings left and continues to gently climb, soon reaching another waymark post, where you turn left off the clear track to climb an extremely pleasant green track up the side of the hill. Take a rest while you are climbing and look over your shoulder, where there are clear views of the

Looking south-west over Pen-y-gyrn, a short distance from Glantwymyn.

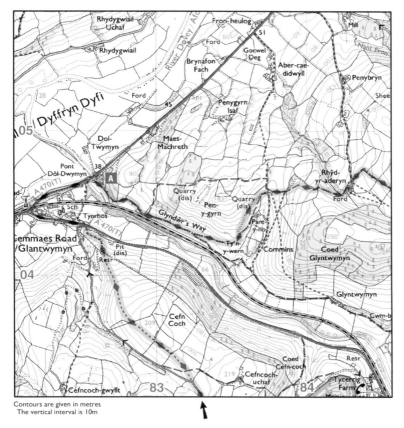

Contours are given in metres
The vertical interval is 10m

hills to the south-west. Continue steadily uphill, ignoring a path off to the left as the track begins an easy descent to a way-mark post. Ignore a gate to your left and walk uphill along the green track, with a fence to your left, to reach another gate.

Go through the gate and, ignoring a faint green hollow track to your left, continue ahead, climbing towards a waymark post. Veer slightly right at the post, walking uphill towards a wooden gate and passing the cornerstone of a long-vanished wall. Go through the gate and continue, veering slightly right. Pass through the next gate and carry on ahead to reach a way-mark post, where you turn left along a clear track beneath Rhyd-yr-aderyn, on a small hill to your right. Continue uphill through a gate, passing a recently renovated farmhouse to your right and barns to your left and turning left as waymarked. After about 20 yards turn right through the second of two gates.

Looking eastwards over Rhyd-yr-aderyn, approaching Commins Gwalia. Soon you will be passing sites ancient and modern: house platforms and a wind farm.

Now walk gently uphill, enjoying fine views across the Dyfi Valley towards Mallwyd, which open up to your left. The track bends sharply right and continues through a gate, and on through a second gate gradually entering more open country-side, redolent of the moorlands traversed in previous sections further south. Go through a gateway as the track swings to the left, passing Gwern-y-Bwlch. Having climbed gently across a field to a gate, you go through and find the views now opening to your right. Go through the gate and carry on, keeping the fence to your left. Go through another gate and continue ahead, crossing rough ground but following a clear track towards a waymark post. As the track swings to the right around the side of the hill there are splendid views ahead of Mynydd y Cemmaes, with the second-generation aero-generators just peeking over the ridge. The summit at the southern end is Moel Eiddew, 1,486 feet (453 metres) high. The track now begins its descent to the road, passing Gwalia (B&B) down to your left, its chimney stack just visible through the trees. Eventually you reach a gate, which you go through to join the road.

Walk ahead along this very quiet road as it at first swings gently right and then continues to a much sharper right turn **B**: here you turn sharp left along a track, as waymarked. Carry on ahead when the track from Bryn-moel joins from the right, now following a much rougher course, which can be very wet during rainy periods. After a gentle climb, a wooden gate appears ahead. Go through this and carry on ahead, keeping the fence on your left, along what is now a wide green track. Descend gently to a gate, go through and turn left along a narrow road. After 100 yards turn right, go through a gate which is set a little back from the road, and proceed ahead along a green track. As you climb, a fence joins your route to the right. Stay on the track as it bends to the right and continues climbing, now quite steeply. When the track splits, continue straight on. Go through a gate and carry on, keeping the fence to your right. There are now expansive views over the Twymyn Valley towards the summit of Corun y Ffridd.

Eventually the undergrowth to your right clears and you can find your way into the hollow lane which follows the edge of the field, with the fence still to your right and absolutely splendid views beyond, with the ubiquitous buzzards overhead. When you reach a gate, go through and continue ahead. Go through another two gates above Fron-gôch and carry on along the track, with a large forestry plantation looming ahead.

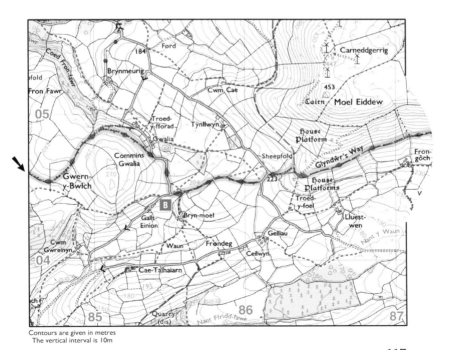

Contours are given in metres
The vertical interval is 10m

117

Another gate is passed as you approach the trees, with the fence to your right, and enter the plantation through a bridle gate.

You are now in Gwern-y-bwlch Forest – a board to your left indicates three waymarked walks should you feel the need for a diversion – where Glyndŵr's Way initially descends to a modest clearing and joins a forest road. Walk to the left, climbing very gently uphill and now following a pleasant forest road – unusually wide, with the trees held well back, and as a consequence unusually light. It's gentle uphill walking, hardly noticeable on the smooth surface. The track climbs to a point where it swings

Looking north from Commins Gwalia towards Snowdonia. Soon the woods will be left behind as you traverse the high hills on this fine section.

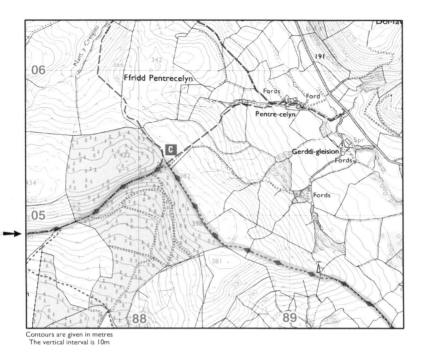

Contours are given in metres
The vertical interval is 10m

away left – just before here look out for a waymark post on the right, which directs you to fork off onto a lesser path between trees, which soon brings you to a bridle gate at the edge of the plantation **C**.

Go through this gate and turn right to walk with the fence and the trees on your right. The view to the north-west is quite magnificent as you overlook the slopes of Mynydd Dôl Fawr and Mynydd Rhiw-Saeson, which enclose the valley of the Nant Rhyd-y-car. Behind you is the Cemmaes Wind Farm. You are now making the last, and very gentle, ascent on this section. Pass through a bridle gate in the field corner and continue with the fence still to your right through a field of rough grass. When you reach the end of the plantation, veer to the left away from the fence, to walk down to reach a field gate in the fence ahead.

Go through this and continue ahead as a transmitter pylon comes into view. Walk towards the right-hand side of this, following the brow of the hill. You are now presented with a stunning panorama as you face the valley towards Talerddig, soon passing through the gate beside the transmitter and continuing downhill along a track with a fence to your left. To the north-east, at the

Welsh weather can, as we all know, be changeable. But sometimes a sight like this, near Cemmaes Road, is more than adequate compensation.

point where two valleys meet, is Plas Rhiw Saeson **36**, the Mansion of the Hill of the English, one of the oldest inhabited houses in the area, dating from the 11th century. This area has a tradition of attracting great poets, and many stayed at Rhiw Saeson. Notable amongst them was Richard Davies, who was born in 1833 and took the bardic name of Mynyddog. He wrote *Sospan Fach* amongst others. Another famous son was Iorwerth C. Peate, who became first curator of the Welsh Folk Museum at St Fagan's, Cardiff.

The track levels out as you approach a gate, which you pass through and continue ahead to reach the concrete road leading to Bryn-aire-uchaf. Turn right here, go through a gate and continue, with a good view of the summit you have just descended to your right and Cwm Pennant dead ahead in the distance. Go through the gate at Brynaere Isaf and continue down what is now a tarmac lane. Carefully cross the railway at the level crossing, following the instructions on the board. When you reach the main road, turn left to reach Llanbrynmair **37**, where you will find the Wynnstay Arms (real ale, food and accommodation), a post office and shop, and the new and quite unique Machinations Museum of Mechanical Magic exhibition and café. This new centre contains wonderful and fascinating hand-made models, continuing the 17th-century Black Forest tradition of clocks featuring mechanical scenes through to the classic age of automata in 19th-century France. Beautifully constructed, they reflect the work of two local village craftsmen, Eric Williamson and Peter Markey, whose 'Timberkits' are sold here. There is also an excellent wholefood café and a shop. It is open every day.

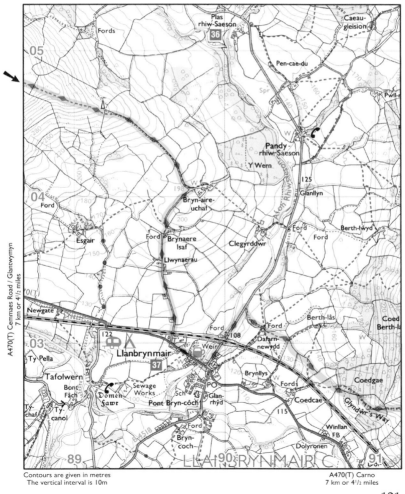

Contours are given in metres
The vertical interval is 10m

A470(T) Carno
7 km or 4¹/₂ miles

Adventures in America

Llanbrynmair has long been known for the number of eminent people – artists, writers, politicians – who have grown up in the surrounding hills. Many subsequently emigrated to America, prompting the Reverend Samuel Roberts, a Congregational minister in the village who was known affectionately as SR, to comment in 1857 in a letter from Cincinnati: 'Of the people born in Llanbrynmair in the last fifty years there are more now living in America than in Llanbrynmair.'

This emigration was more often than not forced upon those who left by unscrupulous landowners in Wales. William Jones described the emigrants' grievances in 1790:

> The hardships which the poor inhabitants of this barren country suffer by the Insatiable Avarice of the Landowners, have affected my feelings so, that I had determined to write too [*sic*] London to get Intelligence of some proprietor of uncultivated land in America in order to offer my services to concert a Plan for removing such of my countrymen as have spirit enough to leave their Aegyptian Taskmasters and try their fortune on the other side of the Atlantic.

In 1856 SR established a company which purchased 100,000 acres of land in Tennessee in order to establish a Welsh settlement there. Unfortunately a series of disputes rendered the scheme unworkable, and the state's involvement with slavery created a moral dilemma for him. Humphrey and Sarah Roberts wrote from Ohio in 1861:

> The Welsh in America have worshiped [*sic*] Samuel Roberts, Llanbrynmair, like Great Diana of Ephesus. He sent a letter here to the North recently, saying that he had swallowed the accursed doctrine of the slave dealers in Tennessee. He says in his letter that the people of the South are more noble and righteous than the people of the North, and that the people of the North are to blame for the conflict, Oh! servant of the enemy and a wolf in sheep's clothing! If he came with his letter, the preachers of the North would give him the coat of tar and feathers which he deserves. Now he is caught in his own trap. It is supposed that he wrote against slavery in Wales and this rises against him now. Enough of the wretch!

Yr Hen Capel in Dolfach, now in the care of CADW. Often the friendly caretaker will let you have a look at its splendid interior.

SR was stung by this wholly untrue criticism, and returned to Liverpool in 1867 during the American Civil War, only to go back to America once more in 1870 in an attempt to sell the land. The failure of this venture was attributed, in part, to the fact that SR was a progressive, a preacher, a thinker, a writer and a reformer – but not a farmer.

12 Llanbrynmair to Llangadfan
Lanbrynmair i Llangadfan

10 ¹/₄ miles (16.5 km)

Leave Llanbrynmair along the minor road to the left of the Wynnstay Arms, signed to Pandy. Continue under the very large stone railway arch, looking out for a signed stile and gate **A** on the right. When you reach this stile, cross it and follow the track uphill, soon passing through two gates. After the second gate turn immediately right, leaving the track to cross over a small plank bridge and another stile (take care, this stile is easily missed). Now walk ahead, initially with the fence to your left, then veer gradually away, ignoring a gate and crossing a stile ahead, just beyond a railway-sleeper bridge over a ditch. Continue ahead, still with the fence to your left, cross a stile followed by a footbridge, before bearing left. Look out for a waymark post, and walk towards it to cross a bridge over a ditch, before veering left towards a conspicuous large tree. Cross the stile beneath the tree and turn left, to walk uphill, with a large gully to your left. As you climb, look out for a waymark post which directs you to bear to the right away from the gully. As you approach a line of hefty old trees look out for a waymark post, which directs you to take the left-hand, grassy, track up the hill, again veering left and still climbing.

Cross a stile and continue along the green track. The main road is at last out of sight and the views to your right are quite dramatic. As the track bears left you reach two waymark posts in quick succession: at the second **B** turn sharp left to follow the rough green track up the hill to reach a fence, where you turn right and continue with the fence and wall to your left, now enjoying a spectacular view over Llanbrynmair, and both the Pennant and Dyfi Valleys.

Soon the track veers away from the wall, and you follow it uphill. Continue ahead, still climbing, when a fence joins from the right. Cross a stile beside a gate and carry on ahead across a field following the very sight indentation which was once a track. Cross a stile and continue ahead.

As you come off the shoulder of this hill look for a stile in the wall ahead. Cross this and veer right to pick up a clear green track. Follow this, skirting the western side of Banc y Gorlan

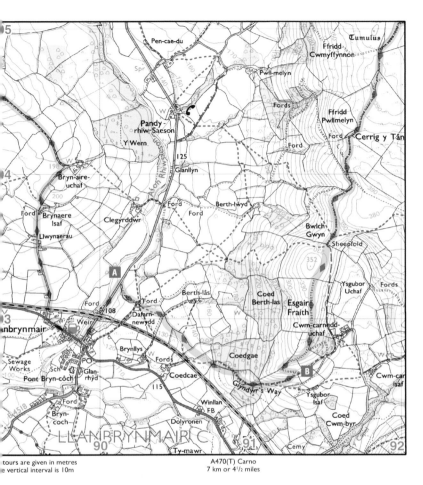

tours are given in metres
e vertical interval is 10m

A470(T) Carno
7 km or 4½ miles

along an old trackway, enjoying quite superb views towards
Mynydd Rhiw-Saeson. When a track joins from the left, continue ahead as indicated on the waymark post. You reach a gate
ahead (ignore the gate to your left), which you go through and
continue along the clear track. Looking towards the south-west,
you can now enjoy an absolutely splendid view of the Pennant
Valley, which culminates at Dylife, passed earlier on Glyndŵr's
Way. Now follow the clear route over Cerrig y Tan. As the track
starts to descend you pass through a gate and turn left, soon
reaching a stile beside a bridle gate. Cross this, pass another
gate to your left (don't go through) and turn right to follow a
clear track towards a forest plantation.

Enter the forest through a gate **C** and continue ahead along the clear track for 1³/₄ miles (2.8 km). Now follow this, passing a reassuring waymark post. When you reach a T-junction, turn left and carry on, keeping a careful watch for a waymark post to your right, which appears shortly after views begin to open up on the right.

When you reach this waymark, fork right off the main forest road down a lesser, but at this point clear, track. When this track divides, bear right as directed by the waymark post. Cross a small ditch and carry on ahead, with the track gradually narrowing and running beside a ditch: it can be wet here, so proceed with care. Finally you cross the ditch to emerge at a gate.

Now leave the forestry and walk ahead and a little to the left, aiming for the right-hand side of a very minor summit and crossing a small ditch. As you approach a fence veer right, to walk

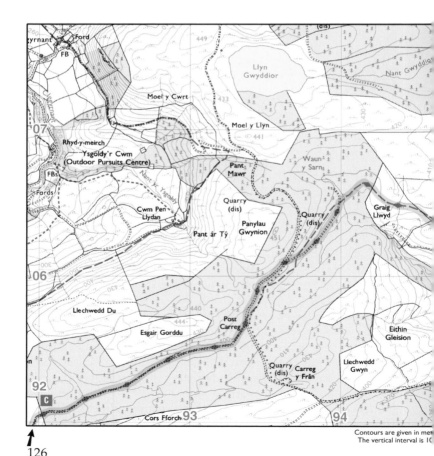

Contours are given in met
The vertical interval is 1(

with the fence to your left. Ignore a gate on the left and continue ahead, soon surrounded by handsome uncultivated moorland. As you approach a junction of three fences, go through a gate on the left, and continue, now with the fence on your right. Soon you join a distinct track, which you follow downhill, enjoying extensive views of the valley and moorland ahead. Stay on the track as it swings to the right and continues its steady descent, still with the fence to the right. Pass through a gate and continue, descending to join a tarmac lane, where you turn left. Stay on this road, which shares the valley with the Afon Gam, ignoring a track off to the right by a cattle grid sign. Pass Neinthirion, with a chapel next door, and stay on the road, crossing the Afon Canno.

When the road swings right at Dolwen **D**, continue ahead. Cross the bridge opposite Dolwen and pass through two gates to

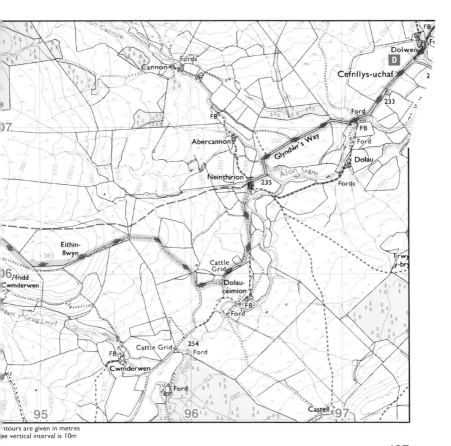

ntours are given in metres
e vertical interval is 10m

leave the farmyard and walk along a track between stone walls. When you reach two gates side by side, pass through the left-hand one and continue along the track, climbing steadily. Pass through a gate and carry on along a beautiful tree-lined lane. Pass through another gate and continue ahead, joining a track which comes in from the right, and follow this, with a fence and trees on the left, until you reach a gate on the left. Go through this and walk along the track. Follow this when it swings left and then right, enjoying superb views. Go through a gate and carry on ahead for about a mile (1.6 km), picking your way through the tussocks of rough grazing towards a waymark post.

Carry on ahead to the next post, and follow the route through a large patch of gorse to reach a more distinct track which heads towards a waymark post on the horizon. Pass this and begin your descent of Pen Coed, walking from post to post, picking your way around the boggy patches while admiring some attractive ponies which roam up here. Continue your descent, bearing to the right and looking out for a fence, then keeping parallel to this. When your descent steepens veer away from the fence and around to the left. Look out for a footbridge **E**, close to a fence at the bottom of the hill. Walk towards this, cross it and climb over the attached stile before turning right to climb a small bank and reach a way-mark post, which directs you to bear left, up the hill. Look out for a

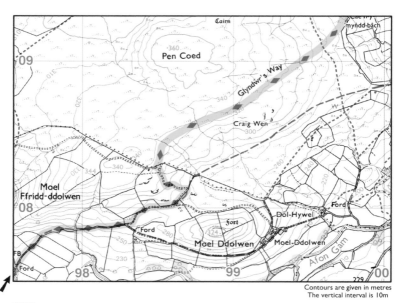

Contours are given in metres
The vertical interval is 10m

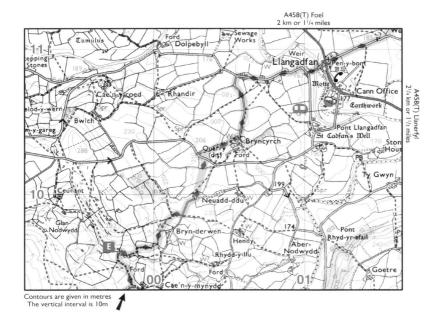

Contours are given in metres
The vertical interval is 10m

waymark post in a gap in a line of trees, and head towards this. Continue as directed to reach another waymark post above a house. Veer left to walk with a fence, and the house, over to your right. Follow the fence until you reach a gate. Go through and walk ahead towards a waymark post on the far side of the field. Cross a stile beside a gate by the post to join a lane and turn left.

Just after the lane swings to the right and gently descends, cross a waymarked stile on the left and walk ahead to a second stile, which you cross. You now cross an area of felled woodland and look for a stile in the bottom right-hand corner. Cross a ditch and the stile and veer right towards another stile and a waymark post at the far side of the next rough and wet field. Cross the stile and turn left to walk along a lane.

After about 50 yards turn right through a gate and follow a track with a hedge to the left to approach Bryncyrch. You can now see Llangadfan ahead. Pass the farm to your right and continue through a wooden gate before turning left. Continue, and when you reach a T-junction, turn right. Just after the road swings to the right, turn left to cross a footbridge over the Afon Banwy, and pass a chapel before reaching the main road at Llangadfan. The excellent Cann Office Hotel, which serves food and real ale in a plain and charming public bar, and offers accommodation, is just a short distance to your right.

13 Llangadfan to Llanwddyn
Llangadfan i Lanwddyn

6 ¹/₂ miles (10.5 km)

Llangadfan takes its name from the Celtic Saint Cadfan, who in the 6th century travelled to Wales from Brittany. A dedicated well lies just to the south – this was saved from being covered by a new road when the Reverend Griffith Howell (1839–63) stepped in. Cadfan was later to become the first Abbot of Bardsey Island. Just along the main road to the south is the handsome Cann Office Hotel, its name thought to derive from Cae'n y ffos, which means a fortified enclosure. This ancient earthwork **38** was built in the 12th century in what is now the hotel's back garden. Take the lane opposite where you emerged onto the main A458 road at the end of the previous chapter and continue ahead, with a red-brick chapel to your left and a handsome stone barn to your right. Continue up the lane, passing an unusual angular wooden building on your left.

When you reach the entrance to Blowty, turn left **A**, go through the gate and walk along the lane until you reach a stile on the right. Cross this and walk around the edge of the field, keeping the hedge to your right. Cross a stile ahead and continue straight

Descending north towards Llanwddyn, and one of the major sights on the route.

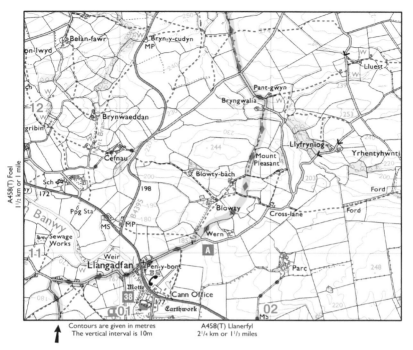

Contours are given in metres
The vertical interval is 10m

A458(T) Llanerfyl
2¼ km or 1⅓ miles

A458(T) Foel
1½ km or 1 mile

across a field to reach another stile. Cross this, cross the track and climb the stile opposite, to walk with trees to your right. Maintain your direction when the trees finish to reach a stile on the far side. Cross this and continue along a long, narrow field. Go through a gate at the far end and carry on with a fence and a hedge to your left. Descend to the corner of the field, cross a stile and a footbridge and carry on, now with the hedge to your right. Climb up the hill, pass through a gate to the right of some sheds to reach a stile. Cross this to join the road and continue ahead, passing Bryngwalia and then Pant-gwyn. When you reach a T-junction, continue ahead, crossing a stile beside a wooden gate and walking with the fence on your left, beyond which there is a pleasant but undramatic view towards Foel. The track is wide enough to have been a drovers' road, part of a network of routes used until the end of the 19th century to bring livestock from the Welsh hills to the markets of London (see page 92). Cross a stile beside a gate and continue ahead, now with the fence and hedge to your right. Carry on gently downhill and, when the fence to your right ends, continue ahead along an old hollow lane with trees, and the remains of a wall, to your left. This track is at times quite boggy.

Lake Vyrnwy: a fine café, and gift shops, are just a short way away.

The track now climbs along a hedged lane to pass through a gate. You maintain your direction along this enclosed track before going through a gate and continuing along the edge of a field, with the fence to your left. Go through a gate to the left of Penyffordd, walk a few paces uphill and pass through a wooden gate to join a road.

Turn left, walk ahead for 15 yards and then turn right **B** along a waymarked forest path, climbing gently. When you reach a clear forest road, turn left as waymarked. After a short while conifers to your left clear to give a wonderful open panoramic view of the Banwy Valley, with gentle rolling hills and mountains beyond. The main summit to the south-west is Pen Coed, rising to 1,180 feet (360 metres). Follow the track as it swings gently to the right and passes a waymark post. Once again you are walking enclosed amidst young conifers, so over the years this track will become increasingly hemmed in. Pass a waymark post and continue ahead as directed. A second post shortly after performs the same function. Now you will find that Glyndŵr's Way has, at least for a while, at last shed its preoccupation with waymarks, changes of direction, gates, stiles and junctions and you can relax and just fol-low a clear track, with little to distract you apart from the fine view at Pren Croes. Another waymark post confirms you are not lost as you press on for 1 ¹/₂ miles (2.4 km), climbing gently.

At a cross-tracks, continue slightly right and ahead to reach a more formally arranged junction of five tracks; here you press on ahead, downhill and to the right. When the main forest road swings around to the right, you continue ahead down a lesser, waymarked, hollow lane, which can be wet. Soon you descend a small dingle amidst tall mature conifers, with the sound of a tumbling stream down to your right. Walk straight across the bend of a forest road, continue down to a gate and go through. Walk straight on, with a fence and trees on your left. Pass a waymarked gate and carry on ahead; then, when the track bends to the right and a stream crosses, ignore the two gates ahead and continue downhill along the track. The going is quite rough here, as the course of a stream shares the lane, and the surface is comprised of small uneven boulders.

Descend to a stream where there is a wooden bridge with a gate, and cross it. Continue ahead along the clear track and, when you reach a lane, turn right **C** as signed. You are now

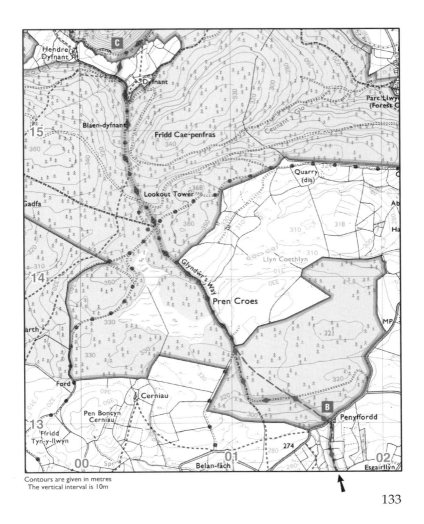

Contours are given in metres
The vertical interval is 10m

walking with tarmac underfoot, along the side of a valley and amidst trees, with a stream somewhere down to your right. A quite substantial hedge eventually replaces the forest to your right, giving the occasional glimpse of the fine view down towards Parc Llwydiarth. Then at last the hedge drops away and the views open. When a forest track forks to the left, ignore it and continue ahead as a second track, from Maesdyfnant, joins from the right. Maintain your direction along what is now a clear road. You descend to pass the entrance to the Lake Vyrnwy Holiday Home Park, then cross a bridge and turn left along a short stretch of rough road to join a better road, maintaining your direction.

Soon you fork right uphill **D** as waymarked. Ignore a track to the right and continue ahead. You continue to a summit where the track forks: take the right fork to carry on more steeply uphill as directed by the waymark post. A little seat on the left provides the opportunity for some respite before you continue this quite substantial climb. You pass the farm of Bryn Cownwy down to the left, which provides visual interest in this quite enclosed valley. At the top of the climb you cross a forest track and carry on ahead along a thankfully less steep incline. Stay on the track as it swings left and then goes downhill.

Eventually you pass a waymark post to emerge at a track junction. Cross straight over the junction and then immediately turn right to climb a stile by a gate **E**, with the dam at Lake Vyrnwy **39** in view ahead. Now walk downhill with the fence to your right. Pass a waymark post and carry on downhill, enjoying fine views over the lake. The small green building you can see is a weather station. A board-walk takes you over a marshy patch to a stile, which you cross and veer right, to walk with the fence to your right. Climb a stile beside a gate and carry on ahead along a track that joins from the right.

There is now an excellent view of the dam, with Pont Cynon beyond and the massive extent of the reservoir hidden away to the left. You descend behind houses to a road and a red telephone box to turn left, passing the old post office. Ignore a path down to the right and continue ahead to the RSPB centre, café, cycle hire and the audio-visual Lake Vyrnwy Experience.

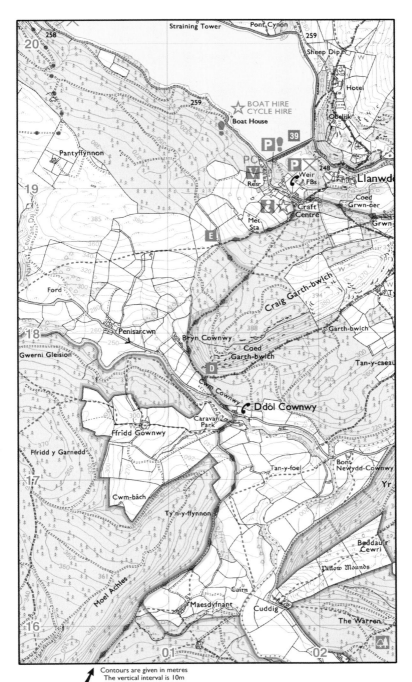

Contours are given in metres
The vertical interval is 10m

The magnificent dam at Llyn Efyrnwy is an impressive site, and has become a major tour

action in Mid Wales.

14 Llanwddyn to Dolanog
Llanwddyn i Dolanog

8 ¹/₄ miles (13.25 km)

Cycles can be hired from the café at Llanwddyn, and it is a level 12-mile (19.2-km) ride around Lake Vyrnwy, if you fancy a break from walking! The RSPB has an excellent shop, and a birdwatching hide. The Lake Vyrnwy 3-D Experience, which opened in 2001, can take you on an exciting virtual tour of the lake, and a separate video will give you an insight into the 24,000-acre (9,712-hectare) Lake Vyrnwy Estate's sustainability and biodiversity. Grazing is restricted in the area to promote re-growth, and there are around 90 species of bird regularly breeding here. The Lake Vyrnwy Hotel, just north-east of the dam, is thankfully open to non-residents. With Sites of Special Scientific Interest, nature trails, a sculpture trail and excellent fishing for brown trout, it is an area worth far more than a fleeting visit.

Having visited Lake Vyrnwy you retrace your steps to the village, passing the old post office on your right **A** and the telephone box on your left to walk along a minor road as waymarked, passing the Coedwig Dderw sessile oak forest. You climb gently to reach a fork in the road, where you go left as waymarked towards Grwn Oer. As the lane climbs gently and swings to the left you veer right to go through a gate at Grwn Oer, ignoring the gate to your left. Continue past the cottage and go through a second gate to walk along a green lane at the edge of woodland.

Pass through the next gate and carry on along the path by the side of the wood, where you might well find yourself completely surrounded by pheasants! Some are inquisitive and come quite close, others panic and flap away through the fence, causing quite a commotion. Leave the fenced track through a gate and turn left to walk downhill along a farm track. Cross a bridge over the Afon Efyrnwy, pass through a gate ahead, walk up to the road and turn right **B**.

Now walk along the broad grass verge, climbing gently and eventually ignoring a track to the right to continue ahead as waymarked. Gradually the view to your right opens up, providing a welcome distraction from the traffic on the road. Ignore a minor road that forks to the right and maintain your direction

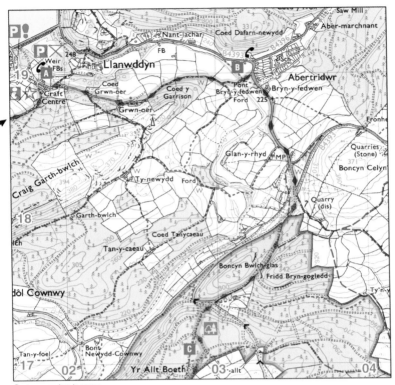

Contours are given in metres
The vertical interval is 10m

towards a waymark post by a wooden bus shelter. Leave the main road and carry on ahead along a minor road to reach a large Forestry Commission sign for Dyfnant Forest, where you fork left through a gate. You now walk along a forest road which climbs gently, still with fine views to the right, and passes an area of felled woodland, with broken trees and brushwood littering the hillside – not particularly attractive but an excellent environment for insects and birds. Continue ahead as waymarked when a track leaves to the left, and carry on to reach a road.

Carry on along the road and shortly turn sharp left **C** up a forest track. After about 60 yards look up to your right for a waymark post marking a rough green track which climbs the hillside through a new plantation. Follow this, passing a waymark post which beckons you to carry on up the hill to reach a second post at a forest road. Turn left here. Continue, eventually stepping around a metal barrier to join a forest road and turn right. A

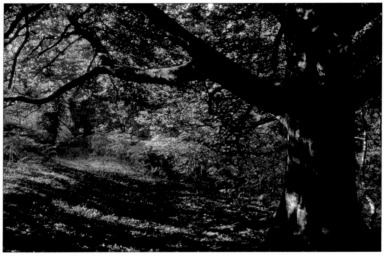

Riverside woodland near Dolanog.

waymark post encourages you to carry on, soon enjoying fine views to the left. When the track bends to the left, look out for a waymark post to the right, which directs you to leave the main track and enter the forest to the right. Continue along this path, which can become quite overgrown with bracken during late summer, soon to reach a stile in a fence by a tumbled stone wall. Cross this and continue slightly right as directed. Cross the brow of the hill and head towards a stile in the fence to your right. The view here is splendid. Cross the stile to enter an area of felled forest and veer left. Descend along a vague path through the remains of the woodland to head towards a stile in the fence at the bottom of the slope. Cross this stile and turn right. Soon veer left and follow the grassy track along the top of the slope. Do not go through the gate by the building ahead, but turn right with the track and descend to a stile beside a gate. Cross this and continue down the track. After about 100 yards you join a track and turn sharp left.

Soon this track peters out and you veer left up a path to a waymark post by a gap in a stone wall. Go through the gap and carry on ahead along a track under mature trees to reach a stile. Cross this and carry on along the hillside, gradually descending and eventually joining a fence to your left. When you reach a gate and a stile, cross the stile and carry on with a stone wall and woods to your right.

Having passed by the remains of some very ancient farm machinery you go through a gate to enter a caravan park. Turn sharp left and walk towards a church. Walk to the left of this, by the green corrugated-iron Llwydiarth village hall to descend to the road, where you pass through a gate and turn right.

At Pont Llogel **40**, where the bridge was built in 1818, there is a prettily situated church standing almost at the edge of Parc Newydd, at one time a medieval deer park enclosing 1,000 acres (2,500 hectares), and owned by the Fychan family. Sir Gruffudd Fychan was an ally of Owain Glyndŵr during the uprising. This is the start of the Pererindod Melangell Walk, a 15-mile (24-km) linear route between the Vyrnwy and Tanat Valleys. It was once used by drovers, quarrymen and pilgrims who visited the church of St Melangell, all that survives of a nunnery built some 1,400 years ago. There is a post office and garage here, both looking very dapper.

Carry on along Glyndŵr's Way, walking below the church at Pont Llogel to reach the Forestry Commission sign for Pont Llogel on your left. Here you turn left **D** just before the bridge to enter the forest. You now walk along an excellent path beside the Afon Vrynwy, through an SSSI rich with oak and hazel, and sharing the route with the Ann Griffiths Bible Walk.

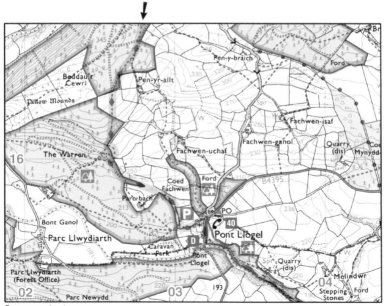

Contours are given in metres
The vertical interval is 10m

Ignore forest walks which are signposted to the left and continue ahead, with the river tumbling over falls through deciduous trees to the right. You pass low rocky cliffs on your left and eventually reach a stile beside a wooden gate by the Vyrnwy. Cross this and carry on with the river on your right, to reach a gated wooden bridge. Cross this and, saying goodbye to the river and the Ann Griffiths Walk, you continue ahead up the bwlch with trees and the stony bed of a stream to your right.

Still keeping the fence to your right, you reach the top of the hill. Here you go through a gate and turn left, continuing with a fence on your left. Climb to a stile in the field corner, cross it and carry on ahead, keeping the ditch to your left. When you reach a stile beside a gate, cross it, cross the road and carry on ahead, through a gate, heading towards Llwyn Hir Farm. You walk along the driveway to the farm, then pass through gates into the farmyard and bear left to cross the yard and leave through a gate, turning right to walk behind the barn to a stile beside a gate. Cross the stile and, ignoring the gate immediately ahead, walk up the track to the left of it, keeping the fence to your right. This very pleasant green track now gently winds its way uphill, with fine views over rolling green countryside to the right. Ignore a rough track which branches off to the left and continue ahead.

From Allt Dolanog looking to the east, before the descent to the village.

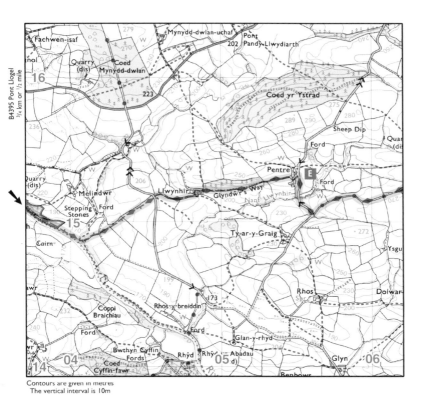

Contours are given in metres
The vertical interval is 10m

When you reach a bridle gate, with a stile beside it, go through and carry on ahead to another bridle gate above a farm building. Go through this and carry on ahead. Pass through a metal gate and turn right, walk through two more metal gates and then veer left to join a road at Pentre Farm **E**.

Turn right along this road and follow it downhill as it descends into a dingle and then climbs, passing a small quarry on the left. When you reach the top of the hill, and the road swings to the right, you turn left along a track as waymarked, resuming your gentle climb. When the track reaches its summit, ignore a gate to the right and carry on ahead to cross a stile beside a gate. Continue ahead and then to the right as a lesser track forks left, then soon swing left to resume your direction. Walk along a wide open track to reach a stile beside a gate. Cross the stile and now walk along a much more enclosed track with trees and bushes on either side. A waymark post reassures you that you are following the correct route.

As you walk along this track look out for a stile beside a gate on the right, below the low summit of Fridd Llwydiarth to the north. Cross this stile **F** and walk with the old fence and hedge to your left. Pass through a gate and continue ahead, crossing a tiny stream. Walk up to a waymark post and continue ahead as directed, with the fence on your right. Ignore a gate to your right, and continue ahead, ignoring a second gate on the right and continuing down to a stile, which you cross and carry on ahead, keeping the fence to your right. There is now a fine view over the Vyrnwy Valley. Carry on to a stile, cross this and turn sharp right to walk with a hedge and a fence to your right. The path descends the field to a stile to the right – cross this and carry on with the fence now to the left. Walk to a waymark post at the edge of a steep slope and turn right to carry on down to a stile at Dolwar Fach.

Cross the stile, climb down to the lane, and turn left. Leave Dolwar Fach through impressive white gateposts with sturdy metal gates, join a road and turn right. Walk along the road for about 30 yards, and then veer off left to cross a stile and walk ahead over common land towards a waymark post on the horizon. The view behind you is quite pleasant, with rolling hills separated by wooded valleys. Eventually you join an old track and continue up the hill as directed by the waymark post, once again sharing the route with the Ann Griffiths Walk. You are now gently climbing the side of Allt Dolanog **41**, which is topped by the banks and ditches of a hill fort. As you continue up the hillside look out for a waymark post to the right, and walk towards this. At the post walk ahead as directed to a further post at the bottom of a bracken-covered slope. You now follow a track which zig-zags uphill, veering left when it forks and passing a waymark post up on the left. Now you find yourself walking along a pleasant green track, soon heading towards a signpost in a dip on the horizon. When you reach the post, fork right off the main track onto a path through bracken. Now stay with the path until a waymark post appears, directing you to carry on ahead through more bracken towards yet another waymark post, to the right of a small knoll ahead, with a splendid view of the Vyrnwy Valley beyond.

The path begins to descend quite steeply through the bracken, passing a waymark post. You eventually emerge from the bracken to join a track and continue ahead. Go through a gate to join a rough tarmac road and continue ahead along this

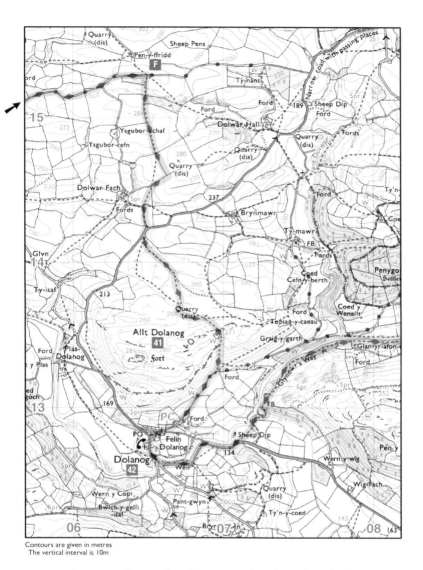

Contours are given in metres
The vertical interval is 10m

extremely attractive valley. You pass the chapel and descend to Dolanog **42** (the dale of the salmon); this was the childhood home of Ann Griffiths (1776–1805), the 18th-century Calvinistic Methodist hymn-writer, who died in childbirth following her marriage to Thomas Griffiths of Meifod. Her family lived at Dolwar Fach. Turn left by the post office, which at one time was the village smithy.

15 Dolanog to Meifod
Dolanog i Meifod

7 miles (11 km)

Leave Dolanog along the main road, passing the church to your right, continuing across the old bridge and ignoring a road which joins from the right. Down to your left, glimpsed through trees, the Afon Efyrnwy tumbles over stones and shallow falls to reach a quite dramatic weir **43**, where the water falls over a sheer drop marking the upstream limit for salmon. Water from these falls once powered a turbine that supplied electricity for the village. The river here is now noted mainly for brown trout, and fish of up to 4 lb (1.8 kg) have been caught. Pass a farm entrance by an old bridge and carry on along the main road as waymarked, still with the river to your left. When the road bends around to the right, you pass a metal field gate and walk up to a stile on the left **A**. Cross this and turn right to walk across a field to a second stile. Climb this and continue ahead with the river still to your left. You now follow what is initially a fine rocky path along the top of a steep defile for almost 2 miles

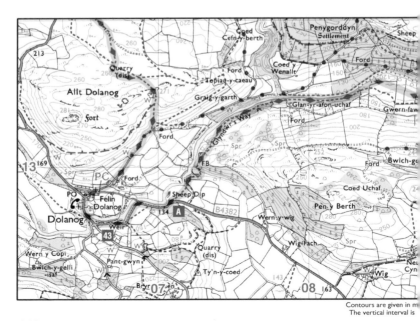

Contours are given in m
The vertical interval is

(3.2 km), passing through dense mixed woodland. You cross a small bridge and a stile, turn left and continue.

When the path temporarily leaves the riverside, follow the waymark posts, crossing a stile and following the path through more old mixed woodland and bracken. Climb a stile through an old overgrown hedge and carry on, soon passing Glan-yr-afon-uchaf to your right, a pretty little rickety cottage.

Shortly after a fence joins your route on the right, you cross a stile and part company with the river, to continue ahead along a rough track and then uphill, passing a small conifer plantation on the left and heading towards Gwern-fawr. When you reach the house veer left along the path and cross a stile to your right before turning left to walk along the lane.

Pass a cattle grid and carry on ahead through mature wood-land, past a second cattle grid, and continue along the clear route – a very pleasant change from the usual intricacies of Glyndŵr's Way. The prominent and distinctive cone-like sum-mit of Bryngwyn appears to the left above the more typical gentle wooded hills of the valley. When a track joins from the left continue ahead, eventually passing the final cattle grid on this lane, to join a minor road **B** and turn left. Soon you turn left to follow the main road at Pontrobert **44**, a village of mainly

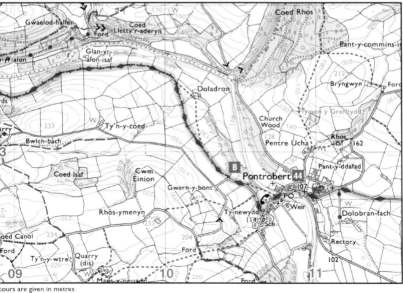

ours are given in metres
vertical interval is 10m

new, and a few not so new, houses, which takes its name from Oliver ap Robert, who built the first bridge here in 1670. Over the centuries the village has supported two iron forges, three grain mills and a woollen factory, along with two grocer's shops, a haberdasher, a cobbler and a blacksmith. Hendafarn, near the bridge, used to be a drover's inn.

The John Hughes Memorial Chapel (Hen Capel John Hughes) and cottage, built in Pontrobert in 1800, was the home for 40 years of the weaver who went on to keep a day school, joined the Calvinistic Methodists and started preaching. Eventually he became a full-time minister at Bala in 1814. His wife, Ruth, was formerly a maid at Dolwar Fach, the home of hymn-writer Ann Griffiths. Ruth read the poems which Ann Griffiths had recited to her, John transcribed them and they were published by the Reverend Thomas Charles in 1806. Each year 12 August is celebrated as Ann Griffiths Day. The fully restored building was reopened in 1995, and there is a programme of day retreats (ring Nia Rhosier on 01938 500631 for details). The chapel is open 14.00–18.00 Tuesday to Friday, and Saturday and Sunday by arrangement. Closed Monday. There is no charge, but donations are welcomed.

Cross the bridge, with the church over to your left, and then turn right towards Meifod and The Royal Oak pub. At the next road junction bear left to pass the pub on your left. Here you can get meals all day, children are welcome, and there is accommodation. When you reach a crossroads by the pretty little red and cream brick chapel Sion, turn right **C** along the ungated road, ignoring a gated track to the right. You pass the entrance to Bryn-y-fedwen and veer right, staying on the track, as waymarked. Cross a stile beside a gate and then walk to the left downhill along a track with a hedge to your left and a pleasant view to your right. At the bottom of the track go through a gate and turn right, ignoring the gates ahead and to your left. Climb a short hill, turn left through a gate and then turn right to walk with the hedge to your right. At the field corner ignore the gate ahead and turn left to walk up the field with the fence and a conifer plantation to your right.

You are now on the brow of a hill, with a view of a gentle valley to your left and trees to your right. Soon you pass a waymark post, and continue ahead as directed. When you reach a stile in the field corner, cross it and continue ahead, with views over the Vyrnwy Valley now opening to your right. Pass through a gateway and walk downhill, with trees and the old Quaker Meeting House to your right. You reach a waymark post and walk to the

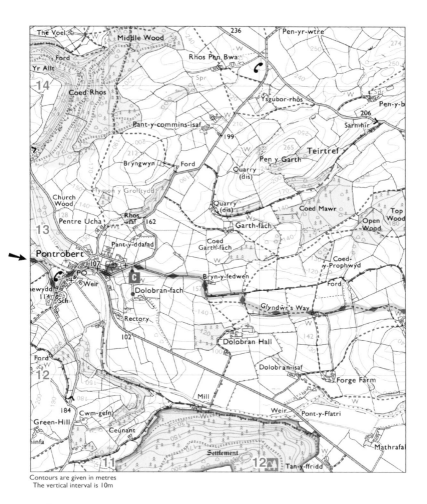

Contours are given in metres
The vertical interval is 10m

right of it to enter an old green lane, which soon swings gently left to reach a stile. Cross this and continue ahead, then climb a stile and cross a bridge in the field corner. Now carry on ahead up the field, with Coed-cowrhyd over to your right. As the fence and the accompanying tidy hedge to your right gradually come closer you will notice a gateway ahead. Go through this and maintain your direction to a second gate by a drinking trough. Pass through this and follow the rough track across the field, passing a waymark post and veering slightly left as directed. Ignore the gateway on your right and continue to reach a stile on your right, which you cross and turn left to walk along the lane.

When you reach a T-junction **D**, turn right to follow a tarmac lane, which winds gently downhill to reach a track entrance on the left. Cross the stile directly ahead of you here and walk diagonally across the field to reach a stile in the opposite corner, by the scant remains of an old hedge. Cross this stile, descend to the lane and turn left to walk uphill between tall hedges. When you reach a junction, continue ahead as directed by a waymark post. Shortly after the lane veers to the right, turn off left **E** over a stile beside a gate and walk over to the fence on the left, to follow the path beside it, ignoring the track directly ahead. A view soon opens up to your left, with a wood to your right. A waymark post at a field

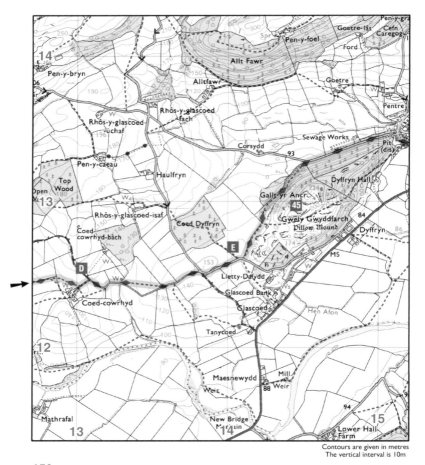

Contours are given in metres
The vertical interval is 10m

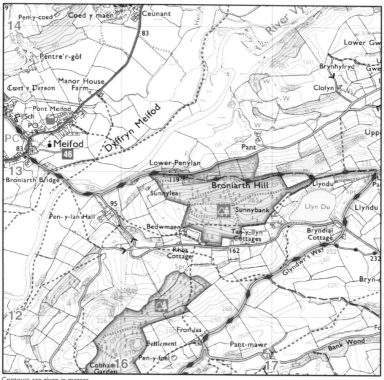

Contours are given in metres
The vertical interval is 10m

corner on your left beckons you to veer left down the field, ignoring two gates on your left and continuing as directed by the waymark. A short stretch of lane brings you to a gate, which you go through and carry on ahead along a hedged green lane. Gallt yr Ancr (Anchorite's Hill) **45**, to your right, has a pillow mound near the top, known as Gwely Gwyddfarch (Gwyddfarch's bed), and is said to mark the last resting place of the saint who founded the church in Meifod around AD 550. Parts of this basic, oak-framed building are thought to have survived until the 17th century, when they were covered by Church Walk. The track then descends beside a thick forest plantation with open views to the left. When you reach a road continue ahead and then, at a T-junction, turn right to walk down to the centre of Meifod **46**, passing the handsome new village hall on the left. You meet the main road opposite the old post office. Turn right to continue the walk.

151

Afon Vyrnwy from Broniarth Bridge, where the local lads from Meifod enjoy a swim durin

summer. Soon you will be zig-zagging south towards Welshpool, and the end of the walk.

16 Meifod to Welshpool
Meifod i'r Trallwng

10³/₄ miles (17.5 km)

Walk past what was once the post office in Meifod, on the left, and then turn left at the road signposted towards Guilsfield, passing a beautifully converted chapel on the right, followed by tennis courts and a bowling green on the left. Cross Broniarth Bridge over the Afon Vyrnwy, in the midst of a wide valley. Stay on the road as it bends gently left, with the buildings of Pen-y-lan Hall ahead, the old stables looking far more charming than the house from this viewpoint. At the next junction turn left to walk along Ffordd Glyndŵr, which climbs gently, with the river down to the left. As you pass the entrance to Pen-lan-isaf look for the track which leaves to the right **A**, and follow this up a steep slope into attractive mixed woodland. When the main forest track hairpins to the right you continue ahead as waymarked. Soon woods become a forest plantation, with regular rows of conifers, as the track continues steeply up Broniarth Hill.

Again, when the forest track swings sharply right, you carry on ahead along a path, continuing your climb and with excellent views over the Vyrnwy Valley opening up to your left. Pass through a gate and carry on ahead, once again walking through mixed deciduous woodland. Go through a gate above a little red-brick hut within an enclosure, and continue ahead, leaving the woodland behind.

Now immediately turn left, as directed by the waymark below a galvanised tank amongst trees, and carry on walking with a fence to your right. Down to your right is Llyn Du **47**. Ignore a gateway on your right and continue up the hill by the electricity poles. When you reach the end of the hedge on the right, turn sharply right to walk down to a gate, which you then go through to join a road, where you turn right **B**.

You now follow this road for a little over a mile (1.6 km), initially getting glimpses of the lake down to your right. Continue straight ahead at a crossroads and walk to Clawdd. Carry straight on when a track joins from the left, still climbing gently. At the top of the incline a very fine view over the Banwy Valley opens to the right and eventually you reach a road junction, where you fork right and walk gently downhill.

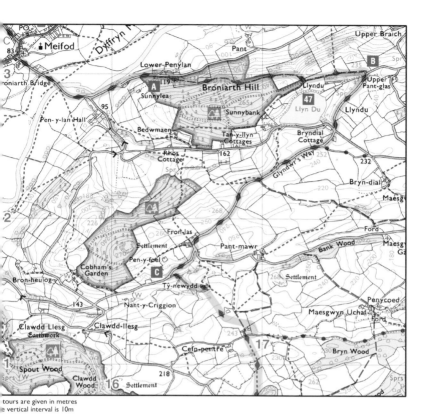

tours are given in metres
e vertical interval is 10m

As the road begins to descend more steeply and swings away to the right, you turn sharp left **C** to cross a stile beside a gate, to walk along a track. Cross a second stile beside a gate and continue ahead as directed by a waymark post: you are now walking across a grassy hill-slope towards trees. Carry on as directed by the next waymark post through a gap in the trees to follow the vestiges of a track towards a gate ahead, overlooked by a corrugated iron barn standing next to the diminutive ruin of Ty Newydd. Go through this gate to walk with a fence to your left. Pass another gate and carry on up the edge of the field with a fence to your left. The path then follows a hedge as it swings gently to the right and you continue towards a well-hidden stile in the corner of the field. Cross this and walk half-right across the field towards buildings, passing by an electricity pole, crossing a diagonal track and continuing towards a stile to the left of the buildings. Cross this and veer right to reach a gate.

Go through this and turn right along an enclosed lane for a short distance. As you emerge from the lane, note the restored buildings of Cefn-pentre on your right before looking for a stile on your left, which you cross.

Now walk ahead as waymarked, crossing the brow of the hill and veering slightly left to pass through a gate and head slightly right to cross a stile beside a gate. Continue, maintaining your direction and climbing gently up towards woods, where a waymark post can be seen.

When you reach the perimeter of the woodland turn right to walk with the fence and the trees to your left, enjoying open views on your right towards Gwely Gwyddfarch, by Meifod. Soon you descend to cross a stile in the corner. Cross this to step down to a road and turn left, following the road as it swings around to the right.

Ignore the entrance to Bwlch Aeddan on your left and carry on up the hill. A waymark reassures you as you pass Pant Pool in the distance to your left. To your right is the Big Forest – a name that flatters. When the road begins to swing to the left, look out for a waymark post which directs you to go through a bridle gate on the left **D** to enter Kennel Wood. Follow the rough path, with a dingle to your left, ignoring a gate to the right, through the trees to reach a stile, which you cross and tend slightly left towards a waymark post, then veering right as directed along an old green trackway below a red-brick house. The track climbs and then turns left by a fence, ignoring a gate ahead. Continue with the fence to your right, overlooking a valley to your left. When the fence swings away to your right, you continue ahead along a track. Carry on along a clear track, pass through a gate and walk ahead, ignoring tracks which leave your route on the left and right. Go through a gate and veer right to walk up the lane, passing pretty landscaped pools and the gardens of a caravan park down to your left. On a hot sunny day the swimming pool here could look very enticing! Follow the lane as it swings to the right, passing the Hidden Valley Chalet Park and continuing up the hill to pass a cattle grid and reach a road, opposite Stonehouse Farm, where you turn right.

Walk carefully along the road, using the verge to avoid traffic, and as you reach the top of the hill, where the main road swings around to the right, turn sharply left by a post box, passing a handsome old red-brick school building with what appears to be a charming little toilet block in the gardens. Pass a disused

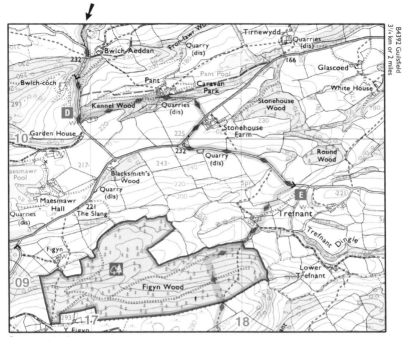

B4392 Guilsfield
3/4 km or 2 miles

Contours are given in metres
The vertical interval is 10m

quarry on the right and continue. Waymark posts reassure you as you walk along the lane until it gently descends and swings to the left: here you look out for a stile on the right **E**. Cross it and walk to the right as directed by the waymark post. Gradually you part company with the fence on your right to reach a way-mark post ahead. Pass through a gap in the trees and carry on diagonally down the field towards a large tree, with the fence over to your right. Walk through a line of trees, then swing left down to a waymark post in front of corrugated iron buildings. When you reach the double concrete farm track follow it for about 10 yards, and then swing around to the left to go through the gate ahead of you. Walk down the field with the fence to your right, and then turn right through a gate at the bottom.

Now walk ahead and, when two gates appear in front of you, don't go through them but turn left to cross over a ditch and a stile beside a gate, then turn right to walk with the ditch to your right.

When you reach a stile beside a bridle gate, cross it and carry on ahead along a path through woodland. You then reach a way-mark post in Figyn Wood, where you turn sharp left. Climb up

157

the steep track through the trees, cross a forest road and continue ahead following a scant line of deciduous trees, stopping now and again to catch your breath and enjoy the view. Leave the wood over a stile and veer half-right, ignoring a gate to your left to walk towards a stile, which you cross and carry on ahead. Ignore waymarks which direct you to the right and, when you reach a gate, go through and continue down the green track until a waymark post directs you to branch off to the right through trees.

When you reach a stile, cross it and continue ahead into Woodland Trust land. This is Graig Wood **48**, an 8-acre (3.25-hectare) wood dominated by sessile oak, with ash, beech, sycamore, crab apple, rowan and field maple. There is hazel, holly, hawthorn and blackthorn in the shrub layer, with bluebells, wood sage, wood anenome, violet, red campion, honeysuckle and primrose at ground level. The woodland is being allowed to regenerate naturally. After about 25 yards turn left as directed by a waymark post to descend to a road, which you cross to reach a stile.

Cross this and walk down the field with a fence on your left. Cross a stile on the left, cross a footbridge, cross a second stile and turn right to walk with a fence and a ditch on your right. As you approach the field corner, veer left towards trees, crossing a small marshy patch. Enter the trees with a fence to your right and then turn right to cross a footbridge over the ditch. Now walk around the edge of the field with the fence and trees to your right. Cross a stile in the field corner to join a road.

Turn right and, very shortly after crossing over a tiny stream, turn left to walk up through trees, climbing steeply over rough ground. Continue, keeping the stream to your left. Cross a stile and continue climbing until the ditch swings to the right. Here you turn left to cross the ditch, climb a stile and continue ahead, with a fence over to your right. Pass a couple of white-painted stiles in the fence, cross an old green lane and carry on until you reach a stile on your right. Cross this and follow the path onto the golf course. Walk uphill along a track, joining the fence on your left through bracken. Descend to a waymark post, which beckons you to veer left, following the line of the fence and crossing a boardwalk over a boggy patch to a waymark post on the far side. When you reach this post, turn sharp right to walk towards the next waymark post, turning sharply left before you reach it. Continue uphill, climbing and veering to the left. You eventually emerge from the bracken and swing left **F** to walk along the side of the hill crest. The view from here is magnificent,

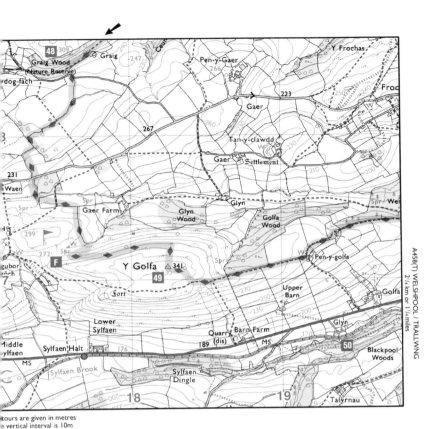

A458(T) WELSHPOOL / TRALLWNG
2¼ km or 1¼ miles

tours are given in metres
e vertical interval is 10m

in a sweep from the north-west to the north-east. Continue along the edge of the golf course, following the waymark posts as they appear, but noting the direction indicated, as you soon have to turn sharply right to climb steeply up the summit of Y Golfa **49** – 1,120 feet (341 metres) high and topped by an Ordnance Survey trig. point. Now the view is equally stupendous, but this time encompassing the whole 360-degree panorama.

Leave the summit as directed by the waymark post and follow the clear green path downhill. When the path splits, go to the right and then bear left downhill, following the posts and entering bracken. Eventually you reach a gate, which you go through and carry on ahead, with a fence and trees to your left. Cross a stile beside another gate and continue ahead. Across the valley to your right is the track of the Welshpool & Llanfair Steam Railway **50**, which opened in 1903, and in the summer you may be lucky enough to see a steam train journeying between Llanfair Caereinion and Welshpool. Go through a gate and carry on ahead, veering slightly left to walk with a broken hedgerow to your right before picking up a track that swings left and then right; soon you are walking with a forest plantation on your left. Go through a gate and carry on along the track. To the left, beyond Wern Wood, is an attractive and very productive area of nursery gardens. Go through a gate and continue ahead with the fence now to the right.

Pass the pond at Llanerchydol Home Farm and walk down to a gate. Go through and carry on descending, passing another pond. Pass a cattle grid by a gate and follow a wide track through parkland by Llanerchydol Hall, eventually joining a tarmac road. Stay on the road as it continues through mixed woodland, passing some magnificently large and gnarled old oak trees – and a well-restored gate-house.

As your descent continues the sound of traffic announces the approach of Welshpool, and soon you are enjoying a fine view over this busy border town. Cross a cattle grid opposite Raven Square Station and fork left to descend to a road, where you turn right. At Raven Square roundabout carefully cross to walk up the road signed to the Town Centre, passing The Raven Inn (food available most days) on your right. Cross the road to walk along the pavement as Raven Street becomes Mount Street. Pass some very enticing pubs as you continue ahead, perhaps taking a look at the restored octagonal cockpit just to the right off the main street. It is thought to be the only one in Wales that survives on its original site. You reach traffic lights by The Royal Oak Hotel. Carry on ahead to pass the Powisland Museum and Montgomery Canal Centre **51**, a traditional wharf and warehouse of about 1880, now housing a museum illustrating the archaeology, history and literature of the local area. It includes a canal exhibition and a display featuring the Montgomeryshire Yeomanry Cavalry. It is open most days, and entry is free. Crossing the Montgomery Canal you arrive at the canalside gardens on your left, where a commemoration stone marks the end of Glyndŵr's Way and the point at which you can loosen your laces and put your feet up for a while.

Welshpool was described in 1822 as being 'a large and populous town', and the appearance of opulence is very predominant throughout the place, perhaps owing to its trade in Welsh flannels, which is carried on here to a very great extent. Originally the streets were lined with smart town houses, backed with gardens, but this ground was soon needed to build

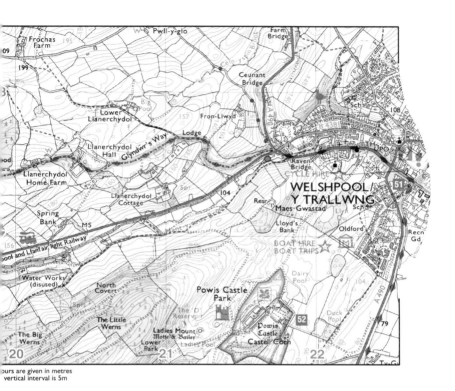

ours are given in metres
vertical interval is 5m

housing for workers who lived, along with their pigs and their
cess pits, in appalling squalor in what were known as 'shuts'.

St Mary's Church is just up the road from The Royal Oak, and
nearby is Grace Evans' Cottage. Grace was the maid of Lady
Nithsdale, a daughter of the Earl of Powis, whose husband, a
Jacobite leader, was being held in the Tower of London in 1715,
awaiting execution. Grace helped Lady Nithsdale rescue her husband, and was given the cottage in recognition of her bravery. A
glacial boulder near the south porch of the church is said to have
been used by Druids.

By the early 20th century Welshpool had become predomi-
nantly a market town, its earlier manufacturing prosperity having faded. Today it is a base for light industry, and during the
summer many visitors come to visit Powis Castle **52** – a
restored medieval castle which has been continuously inhabited for over 500 years. On display are fine paintings, tapestries,
early Georgian furniture and relics of Clive of India. The 18th-
century terraced gardens are superb.

161

The Montgomeryshire Canal

Glyndŵr's Way reaches its end in a garden beside the canal bridge in Welshpool, where it links with the Severn Way regional route. Just the other side of the bridge there is Welshpool Lock and the Powisland Museum.

The opening of the Montgomeryshire Canal in 1796 contributed greatly to the town's prosperity, and eventually the Shropshire Union Canal Company made Welshpool the administrative centre for their Welsh region, and an extensive group of buildings was erected around the wharf in Severn Street, enclosed by a sandstone wall – built perhaps to spare the aristocratic eyes of the Earls of Powis the sight of this industrial activity. A terrace of these buildings is still standing and, if you peep through the window of the house closest to the road, you can see the clerk still keeping his ledger up to date. The cottage next door was originally a salt warehouse, later to become the lock-keeper's cottage. No. 3 was a joiner's shop, No. 4 was the residence of the owner of a local corn-mill, and No. 5 was a house and warehouse. The Powisland Museum occupies what was once a granary/warehouse. The old canal maintenance yard is now occupied by a builder's merchants, and once contained a small internal railway system.

When the mainline railway came to Welshpool, trade on the waterway dwindled, and it closed in 1944 following a disastrous breach in 1936 at the Perry Aqueduct, near Frankton. Since the 1960s there has been an energetic campaign for its eventual restoration, and this now seems assured of success. A trip boat operates from the wharf during the summer, cruising as far as Berriew – ring 01938 553271 for details.

PART THREE

Useful Information

Transport

Rather than give details of a whole raft of individual bus companies and timetables, which will almost certainly be out of date by the time you come to use them, we can do no better than recommend the *Powys Travel Guide*, obtainable from Tourist Information Centres in Powys (see opposite), which covers the entire route of Glyndŵr's Way. This gives complete, up-to-date details of services and timetables, and includes a detailed map which marks Glyndŵr's Way superimposed on the public transport routes, making it very easy to check the links. The Helpdesk number is 0845 607 6060.

Traveline Cymru. For details of buses ring 0870 608 2608, the service is available from 07.00 to 21.00 every day.

A Freedom of Wales Flexi Pass gives unlimited access to Wales bus and train services – telephone 0870 9000 777 or visit www.walesflexipass.com

RAILWAY SERVICES

Wales & Borders Trains
The Heart of Wales Line
This exciting railway, which links Shrewsbury with Swansea, has stations at Knighton and Llangunllo at the southern end of Glyndŵr's Way. Details and train times can be obtained from the Heart of Wales Travel Centre: telephone 01597 822053, and at www.heart-of-wales.co.uk

You can buy tickets online at: www.qjump.co.uk and www.thetrainline.com

The Cambrian Line
There are stations at Machynlleth, the hub of Glyndŵr's Way, and Welshpool, at the end of the walk, on the line linking Shrewsbury, Aberystwyth and Pwllheli. Train times can be obtained on 08457 484950, and at www.walesandborderstrains.co.uk, where you can also book tickets

For National Rail Enquiries ring 08457 484950 (Welsh language: 0845 60 40500).

Accommodation

Powys County Council produces a free list of quality assured accommodation, inspected and graded by either the AA, RAC or Welsh Tourist Board, which is obtainable from Tourist Information Centres on the route (see below). Information on this accommodation is also available at: www.brilliantbreaks.roomcheck.co.uk or ring: 01654 703526.

Coverage on this list is, however, a little patchy and you can widen your scope by visiting: www.talbontdrain.co.uk for a list of other reputable B&Bs and guesthouses who choose not to participate in the above scheme.

It is well worth planning and booking your accommodation in advance, as you will almost certainly have to resort to a form of motor transport (taxi or a lift) to get you to and from your accommodation at some stage of the walk. A mobile phone will prove invaluable for organising this. There are very few camping opportunities, and no Youth Hostels, on the route.

Celtic Trails offer a complete walking package for the length of the trail, including accommodation, luggage transfer and railway station collection. They can also organise short walking breaks along sections of the trail. Contact: Celtic Trails, PO Box 1, Chepstow, Monmouthshire NP16 6ZD. Telephone: 01600 860846. Email: info@walkingwales.co.uk Web: www.glyndwrsway.com

Two websites also have details of some accommodation relevant to Glyndŵr's Way: www.activitywales.com, and www.midwalesindex.co.uk

Tourist Information Centres

Knighton: Offa's Dyke Centre, West Street, Knighton, Powys LD7 1EW. Tel: 01547 529424.
    Email: oda@offasdyke.demon.co.uk
Welshpool: Vicarage Garden, Church Street, Welshpool, Powys SY21 7DD. Tel: 01938 552043. Email: weltic@powys.gov.uk
Machynlleth: Canolfan Owain Glyndŵr, Maengwyn Street, Machynlleth, Powys SY20 8EE. Tel: 01654 702401.
    Email: mactic@powys.gov.uk

Useful Addresses

British Trust for Ornithology, The Nunnery, Thetford, Norfolk
IP24 2PU. Tel: 01842 750050. Email: info@bto.org
Web: www.bto.org

Countryside Council for Wales(CCW)/Cyngor Cefn Gwlad
Cymru, Maes-y Ffynnon, Fford Penrhos/ Penrhos Road,
Bangor, Gwynedd LL57 2DN. Tel: 01248 385500.
Email: bangor@ccw.gov.uk Web: www.ccw.gov.uk

Glyndŵr's Way National Trail Officer, Powys County Council,
Canolfan Owain Glyndŵr, Heol Maengwyn, Machynlleth,
Powys SY20 8EE.
Tel: 01654 703376. Fax 01654 703381.

Mid-Wales Tourism, The Station, Machynlleth, Powys SY20 8EG.
Tel: 0800 273747. Fax: 01654 703855.
Email: info@brilliantbreaks.demon.co.uk
Web: www.brilliantbreaks.roomcheck.co.uk

Montgomeryshire Wildlife Trust, Collot House, 20 Severn
Street, Welshpool SY21 7AD. Tel: 01938 555654.
Fax: 01938 556161.
Web: www.montgomeryshirewildlifetrust.co.uk

National Trust Office for Wales, Trinity Square, Llandudno,
Gwynedd LL30 2DE. Tel: 01492 860123. Fax: 01492 860233.
Email: enquiries@thenationaltrust.org.uk
Web: www.nationaltrust.org.uk

Ordnance Survey, Romsey Road, Southampton, Hampshire
SO16 4GU. Tel: 08456 050505 (Welsh language: 08456 050504).
Fax: 023 8079 2615.
Email: customerservices@ordsvy.gov.uk
Web: www.ordsvy.gov.uk

Powys County Council [HQ], County Hall, Llandrindod Wells,
Powys LD1 5LG.
Tel: 01597 826000. Email: tourism@powys.gov.uk
Web: www.powys.gov.uk

Powys County Council [Montgomeryshire], Severn Road,
Welshpool, Powys SY21 7AS.
Tel: 01938 551000. Email: tourism@powys.gov.uk
Web: www.powys.gov.uk

Ramblers Association, 1 Cathedral Road, Cardiff CF11 9HA.
Tel: 02920 343535. Fax: 02920 237817.
Email: beverleyp@ramblers.org.uk
Web: www.ramblers.org.uk

Royal Society for the Protection of Birds, The Lodge, Sandy,
Bedfordshire SG19 2DL. Tel: 01767 680551.
Web: www.rspb.org.uk
Wales Tourist Board, Brunel House, 2 Fitzalan Road, Cardiff
CF24 0UY. Tel: 029 2049 9909. Fax: 029 2048 5031. Email:
info@tourism.wales.gov.uk Web: www.wtbonline.gov.uk
Weathercall (Meteorological Office) 09068 232 784.
Web: www.weathercall.co.uk

Bibliography

Barber, Chris, *In Search of Owain Glyndŵr*, Blorenge Books, 1998.
Bick, David E., *The Old Metal Mines of Mid-Wales*, The Pound
House, 1977.
Davies, David Wyn, *The Town of a Prince*, Machynlleth Rotary
Publishing, 1991.
Doughty, A., *The Central Wales Line*, Oxford Publishing, 1997.
Godwin, Fay & Toulson, Shirley, *The Drovers Roads of Wales*,
Wildwood House, 1977.
Hughes, Stephen, *The Archaeology of the Montgomeryshire Canal*,
RCAHMW, 1983.
Ifans, Rhiannon, *Owain Glyndŵr, Prince of Wales*, Y Lolfa, 2000.
Jones, Rab, Perrott, David & Richards, Mark, *Glyndŵr's Way*
(sixteen leaflets), Powys County Council, 2000.
Moore-Colyer, Richard, *Roads & Trackways of Wales*, Landmark,
2001.
Morris, Jan & Morys, Twm, *A Machynlleth Triad*, Viking, 1993.
Powys Montgomeryshire Federation of Women's Institutes, *The
Powys Montgomeryshre Village Book*, Countryside Books,
1989.
Powys Montgomeryshire Federation of Women's Institutes,
Montgomeryshire Memories, PMFWI, 1994.
Remfrey, Paul Martin, *A Guide to Castles in Radnorshire,*
Logaston Press, 1996.
Shaw, Joan, *Mostly Montgomeryshire*, Brewin Books, 1992.
Skidmore, Ian, *Owain Glyndŵr, Prince of Wales*, Christopher
Davies, 1978.
Stone, Moira K., *Mid Wales Companion*, Anthony Nelson, 1989.
Trant, Ion & Griffith, Michael Wynne, *The Changing Face of
Welshpool,* The Powysland Club, 1998.
Twigg, Aeres, *Owain Glyndŵr*, Gomer, 2000.

Ordnance Survey maps covering Glyndŵr's Way

Explorer (1:25 000) 201, 214, 215, 216, 239
Outdoor Leisure (1:25 000) 23
Landranger (1:50 000) 125, 126, 135, 136 and 137 or 148